Facing Death

An Interdisciplinary Approach

Edited by

PAUL BADHAM and PAUL BALLARD

D0493678

UNIVERSITY OF WALES PRESS
CARDIFF
1996

© The Contributors, 1996

British Library Cataloguing-in-Publication Data.
A catalogue record for this book is available from
the British Library.

ISBN 0-7083-1331-0

Cover design by John Garland, Pentan Partnership, Cardiff
Typeset by Action Typesetting Limited, Gloucester
Printed in Great Britain by Dinefwr Press, Llandybïe

Contents

Part II   The Quest for Meaning and Purpose in Death

Preface

The initiative for this book came out of a conversation between the editors on the need to encourage cross-disciplinary discussion between the different professional groups dealing with issues concerning death in our society. Enquiries elicited an immediate response from those who formed the core group representing palliative medicine, law, social work, philosophical ethics, systematic and practical theology. Out of the early discussions the shape of the book gradually emerged. Other contributors were subsequently invited.

The aim is for contributors to talk out of their personal research and interest about the issues surrounding death in such a way as to enable others from different perspectives to understand them. It is hoped thereby to provide, especially for students, both in general education and in specialist training, a cross-reference book, so that they can see the field more widely and appreciate how others look at the same problems. It is impossible to cover every aspect of so wide a topic but, we believe, most of the key dimensions are covered.

The editors would like to express their appreciation of the help and co-operation given by all the contributors and others who were part of the process. We have all learned much from each other. Also thanks are due to those who helped get the text together, typists and secretaries and, not least, the University of Wales Press and their editorial staff.

Paul Badham
Paul Ballard
January 1996

List of contributors

Paul Badham is professor of theology at University of Wales, Lampeter, where he is co-director of the MA programme in Death and Immortality. He has written extensively on this subject.

Paul Ballard teaches practical theology at University of Wales, Cardiff, with a main academic interest in church and pastoral care in contemporary society.

John Daniel teaches philosophy at University of Wales, Lampeter.

Andrew Edgar teaches philosophy at University of Wales, Cardiff. His main interest is in social and ethical issues, including working at a European level on the notion of measuring the indices of the quality of life (QALYs).

Peter Fenwick is a consultant psychiatrist at the Maudsley Hospital in London, and president of the British board of the International Association for Near-Death Studies.

Elizabeth Fenwick is currently researching near-death experiences.

Ilora Finlay is consultant in palliative medicine and honorary senior lecturer in the University of Wales College of Medicine; medical director, Holme Tower Marie Curie Centre, Penarth, South Glamorgan; and chairman of the Ethics Committee of the Association for Palliative Medicine for Great Britain and Ireland.

Mervyn Lynn teaches law at University of Wales, Cardiff, specializing in medical law.

Heather Snidle taught social work in the School of Social and Administrative Studies and Pastoral Care in the Department of Religious and Theological Studies at University of Wales, Cardiff, with a special interest in pastoral care in relation to HIV and Aids.

Stephen Williams is professor of systematic theology at the Union Theological College, Belfast, having previously taught theology at the United Theological College, Aberystwyth, and worked at the Whitefield Institute, Oxford.

1
Facing death: an introduction

PAUL BADHAM AND PAUL BALLARD

Death is the one inevitable human fact. We all have to die at some time. But death is never simply a biological event, the cessation of a particular life. It is always more than that, for death is part of our human experience and therefore we have always to try to make sense of it. The great absurdity, that which crosses all existence, is thereby the great question: what do we make of death? This has always been so. The earliest real evidence of human existence seems to have included some kind of reverence of the dead, and religious survival rituals. Cave man was struggling with the meaning of being a sentient spirit whose time came to an end. And such questions continue to be asked: how do we deal, personally and as a society, with the reality of human death?

In the latter years of the twentieth century, however, these questions have taken on new dimensions. Indeed we are facing questions our ancestors could never have dreamt of. We are heirs to the amazing achievements of human science and technology that enable medical processes to protect and renovate the body. Simply put, many erstwhile life-threatening conditions can now be more and more controlled or overcome. But these have brought with them new ethical questions, questions with which this and subsequent generations have continuously to grapple. There are no easy answers concerning matters of life and death. Perhaps it is true to say that the new situation is this: having been so successful in so many ways in prolonging life, we now have to face the question of when we let people die. Such a question arises in many forms and in different situations.

At the basic level there is the need to know when death has occurred. Biological death is a complex process that can take place over quite a prolonged period. Indeed it is true that we start to die from birth. But it is also obvious that humans can survive without the use of different organs. It is also observable that parts of the body cease to function in the course of dying at different times. In the end, death finally occurs only when the body has ceased to have sufficient order for enough parts to function together as a coherent whole. In other words, biological death is a condition of chaos, the breakdown of the system. At the heart of this, however, is that which seems necessary for any kind of life. The ultimate point of disintegration is brain-stem death. 'The brain stem definition of death assumes that human death involves the loss of a critical irreplaceable system essential to the integrated life of the organism as a whole.'[1] But even then this does not necessarily happen in an instant. It is also possible to sustain bodily activity after the body ceases to be able to care for itself. Only when the tissue is irretrievably damaged is the process irreversible, though this will normally be only a few minutes after the supply of oxygen has ceased. With the sophisticated medical skills available to us, it is increasingly possible to reverse a process which only a few years ago, once started, would have had to run its course. The boundary between life and death has become very thin.

Such a situation has had a knock-on effect. As people approach death, and more and more of them are increasingly frail and elderly, so the processes of dying have been prolonged. Mind and body generally become less responsive. In some cases it would appear that a person has entered a living death. With greater pressures on resources for health care, there is constant anxiety about how far it is right to keep people, otherwise totally dependent, alive. At the same time, rising expectations mean that death for the young or comparatively young is thought of as tragic, cutting a life off short that could perhaps have been saved.

These, then, are the questions addressed in the first part of the book. It is not possible within the limitations of space to take up every aspect or to relate to every concerned profession. The chapters are of three sorts. Paul Ballard and Andrew Edgar discuss the social pressures exerted by modern longevity. Mervyn Lynn, Ilora Finlay and Heather Snidle look at the dilemmas and tasks facing three key groups of people: the lawyers who are exercised in interpreting and creating the legal framework within which life-and-death decisions are made; the doctors and nurses and other medical staff who have the responsibility of caring for those who are dying; and the social workers and counsellors who work with individuals and families who face death either for themselves or in relation to those they love. In all these cases the central focus is not on the biological reality but on persons, people going through, and trying to come to terms with, the mystery of being human, whether as those who have to take professional responsibility or as those for whom it is literally a matter of life and death. All these discussions raise the question of controlled forms of euthanasia. Paul Badham and Stephen Williams present cases, both from a religious point of view, for and against the legalization of the practice of euthanasia.

In part II the emphasis shifts towards the philosophical and religious issues posed by death and dying. Is death the end? Is it just the ultimate absurdity, or can we use our mortality as a creative part of living? But what if death is not the end? Perhaps there is something more, so that death, in all its tragedy, is but a frightening gateway to something else. Shakespeare talks about 'death – the undiscovered country from whose bourne no traveller returns'.[2] So is all speculation, a guess, hazarded on faith? Or are there signs and signals that suggest it may be more than wishful thinking.

Peter and Elizabeth Fenwick share with us their researches into the experiences of those who have appeared to die. Of recent years there has been a considerable interest in the 'near-death experience'. Some have found this as evidence for life beyond death. Paul Badham discusses the more traditional basis for various religious beliefs in immortality and how these impinge on an understanding of death. Andrew Edgar bases a discussion of death as giving meaning to life on the thought of the German existentialist philosopher Martin Heidegger; while John Daniel offers another philosophical approach, looking at our cultural consciousness of death and how the event of death, how a person dies, can give a perspective to a person's life.

All these contributors, whether more descriptive or deliberative, gather round the ethical issues concerning death in today's society. These are of the utmost importance for our future together. Some see the choices before society as a possible watershed. The pressures towards accepting the need to decide matters of death as well as life are seen as a dangerous boundary that should not be crossed. Others, however, recognize the responsibility that is being laid on people and institutions but see it as something that must be accepted creatively. Indeed there is promise of a new freedom that can enrich our lives together. These things are not easy. Nor will any new social consensus emerge quickly or without controversy. Rather, we are going to have to continue to absorb technological and social changes. What this will mean only time will tell. It will also depend on those cultural vehicles of meaning, of which religion has traditionally been the most important, which inform and shape our attitudes. There is a symbiotic relationship between these. The changes in society influence how we perceive reality while, at the same time, what we believe shapes what we do. It is hoped that these chapters will help forward this difficult debate by placing it in a cross-disciplinary and multi-professional context. All too often different interested parties wrestle with such issues without recognizing that others are similarly engaged and may have insights and experiences that can illuminate the situation. If this book enables some greater interdisciplinary understanding and discussion it has done its task.

Notes

1 D. Lamb in A. V. Campbell, *Dictionary of Pastoral Care* (London SPCK, 1987), 62. See also Hon. Secy., Conference of Medical Royal Colleges and their Faculties, 'Diagnosis of Brain Death', *British Medical Journal*, 13 (November, 1976), 1187–8; and S. B. Nuland, *How We Die* (London, Chatto and Windus, 1994).
2 *Hamlet* III.i.

Part I
Issues raised by Recent Advances in the Prolongation of Life

2
Intimations of mortality: some sociological considerations

PAUL BALLARD

We each have to die our own death, wherever and however it comes. No one can go through it with us. In many ways it is the most private of all events. Yet, paradoxically we never die in isolation but as part of a community, a member of society, however rich or impoverished those relationships may be. How death is met, understood and dealt with practically, arises from the social patterns and perceptions that inform that society. The dying and those around them, family, friends, carers and others, are part of a common experience and shared expectations, even while recognizing that each person is a particular case. Through history and across the world, different cultures have perceived death in different ways. Those who are ageing and dying have been given different kinds of treatment, from honour to rejection. Economic, technological, political and social factors have shaped the way death is coped with. Our own society is no exception. Indeed it has perhaps seen more and greater changes in this area than any previous age.

The aim of this chapter, therefore, is to explore some of the ways in which our society deals with death and dying. It is thus primarily an attempt to indicate issues raised from a sociological perspective. The sociology of death is a comparatively undeveloped field, though there is at present a growing, lively interest and a rapidly expanding literature. What Gorer called the modern taboo subject is rapidly being recognized as being of central human significance.[1] However, all that can be done here is to point to certain key trends and indicate some areas of debate.

There is, however, another concern that informs this discussion:

the interests of pastoral care. There is a growing recognition that the pastoral care of the dying and their nearest and dearest is a very important dimension of geriatrics. As people grow old and get even nearer death, so they need the support of those who, whether as nurses, doctors, counsellors or case workers or in a more general way, as family, friends and neighbours, understand something of the journey being undergone. But pastoral care must be informed by sociology as well as psychology. In the process of trying to provide an interdisciplinary overview, this book is bound to be concerned with the major and immediate socio-ethical issues facing society in this field. But these can occupy too much attention and be debated within too narrow a perspective. Those who are helping people to negotiate this minefield with creative sensitivity also need to recognize the wider context against which issues such as euthanasia are discussed. To do this we need some indication of how death is regarded in our society, and how those moving into old age tend to view the approach of death, as well as what it means to deal with death directly as patient, relative, friend or carer.

1 Demographic changes

People are, on average, living longer. Of this we are all aware, and it has no need to be documented in detail here. For example, in 1910 the average length of life of British men was 51.5 years, and women 55.4 years (not much greater than that for Africa today – 49.7 years); by 1980 the British average was 73.7 years, and it continues to rise. This must mean a proportionate increase in the numbers of the elderly, many more living well into their late eighties and nineties. Of deaths recorded in 1969, 29 per cent were of people under 65 years of age; 31 per cent of people aged 65–74; and 40 per cent of people over 75. In 1987 the proportions had changed: 22 per cent under 65; 23 per cent between 65 and 74; 55 per cent over 75, with an increase of this last figure of 15 per cent in eighteen years.[2]

The increase in longevity is due to two interrelated factors. Most importantly, there have been real reductions in the mortality rates for mothers in childbirth, infants and young children. The early years are no longer a hazard, even though the first year is still a comparatively dangerous time. Approximately 1 per cent of all deaths annually are of infants, though 80 per cent of deaths are of those over 65. Secondly, improved diet together with changed social and working conditions have enabled people to live longer, and these factors are supplemented by massive medical advances, from the control of the traditional killer diseases such as measles, TB, cholera, smallpox to the ability to provide organ transplants and modern treatments that are taken for granted today.

Such a shift is clearly fundamental both to the make-up of society and its structures and to our understanding of death. Many of the implications will be drawn out at other points, but here it is important to underline one.

Death, other than in exceptional circumstances, normally comes after a reasonably long life. Almost any life-threatening situation will be coped with. In earlier generations it may have been true that death was a constant threat, a dreaded visitor to every household. This certainly did not make grief any less real, but death was a normal part of existence to be accepted with patience.[3] In our situation, however, death before the due time is all the more difficult to deal with. The death of a child, for instance, is comparatively unusual and therefore harder to account for. There is often a feeling that it could have been prevented. Resentment and anger are directed against those who should have known what to do. In a litigious society there is a more ready recourse to law. It must, however, be wondered if the social condoning of such emotions is beneficial and prevents a healthy resolution of the grief process. This is not to deny the legitimacy of apportioning blame where it is clearly necessary; but grief also requires the possibility of reconciliation and acceptance. Long legal battles and media hype do not always seem therapeutic. Emotional reactions to early death focus on what might have been, the lost years and talent. This, too, makes it harder to shut the door creatively on the past. Even those who die soon after retirement are thought of as dying young. Retirement itself, given present-day normal life expectancies, is thought of less as a relief after years of toil than as a new future, an extended period of self-motivated activity.[4]

The result is to push death more onto the margins of social consciousness. It is there, but only comes later. It is there but not often encountered. Many will not come into close contact with death until early adulthood, and even then it is the death of grandparents or even great-grandparents who may well have been fairly distant figures. Death is only expected as the fitting, if necessary, end of a long life, indeed when one has become frail and inactive. Thus death is often regarded as a merciful release from struggling on. In any case, it seems to be assumed, the older generation has had its day and is no longer an active part of society. Death is what happens to marginalized people on the margins of society.[5]

2 The medical professions

Inevitably the medical professions are involved in the matter of death. On the one hand, they are in charge of most of the institutional structures that care for or monitor those who are dying. On the other, they are those who make available to the public the benefits of modern medicine which has done so much to extend life and improve its quality. A number of points need to be briefly noted.

First, the very success of medicine has brought its own problems. Modern society seems to have an innate belief in the power of science and technology. Doctors, especially, are regarded as part of that élite, members of what Langdon Gilkey called 'priests in white coats'.[6] This puts an enormous pressure onto a profession to live up to expectations or lose public status.

Secondly, and connectedly, the medical professions sit on the frontiers of life and death, but the commitment is to cure rather than to care. R. A. Lambourne has pointed out that the cutting-edge of medical services is at the point of high technology, specific diagnosis and clear, positive outcome.[7] The ideal figure is the surgeon. There is, therefore, a strong pull towards the curative model. This is caught by other parts of the medical world. Nursing, for instance, while committed to caring, is still primarily focused on getting people better and sending them home. To admit that effective treatment is no longer possible is something like admitting defeat. It is thus too easy to set aside the incurable and dying as of no importance, thus furthering their 'social death'. Over the past two or three decades, however, the caring dimension has begun to be taken seriously, not least through the pioneering activities of the hospice movement. Palliative medicine is now a recognized element on the medical curriculum. Yet it is still true that the old models are strongly entrenched.[8]

Thirdly, part of this dilemma has been the increasingly technological nature of medicine, not least in those areas that most affect the elderly and dying. Methods of life support and the means of recovery from radical surgery demand highly complicated machinery, to which the patient is variously and firmly attached. This certainly can come between the patient and other people. It can also have the effect of reducing the patient effectively to a machine. Indeed, in the extreme, but for comparatively few people, life of any sort is only possible on the basis of various life-support machines. Apart from any questions about control over these pieces of equipment and who switches off, which will be considered in other chapters, there is always a depersonalizing effect, enhancing dependency and inhibiting interpersonal relationships.[9]

Fourthly, however, it is perhaps simply the fact of institutionalization that poses the biggest problem. It is true that we are now more sceptical of large institutions, but it is still the case that economies of scale can make limited resources available to more people. Highly sophisticated equipment can only be managed through a hospital. Equally, for instance, expert or intensive nursing care is more economically provided through institutional means. But large and busy organizations, especially if they are managed and judged in market terms of quantative throughput, tend to dehumanize, demanding from already vulnerable people, including the elderly, dependency and helplessness. It is also more efficient to bring together those with common needs. So, for example, long-term elderly patients are found on their own wards, cut off from other kinds of patient, with only each other as companions, which compounds the problems of social isolation and marginalization. Moreover, morale of staff and patients is important. Such long-term, often unrewarding forms of caring can be very demoralizing. Too often such routine tasks are allocated to those less highly skilled. To maintain professional standards calls for high levels of commitment and dedication. Also, even where it is expected, as it must be in such an environment, death is seen as a necessary evil, not something to be too openly acknowledged, but covered up and pushed aside lest others be upset and depressed.[10]

The medical professions, through their skills and the structures of modern medicine, are, therefore, caught up in and contribute to the shaping of modern attitudes to death. Death is indeed 'the last enemy', but that makes it all the more difficult to handle that reality positively and creatively.

3 The nuclear family

British family patterns are very complex and take many different forms.[11] But the predominant model is that of the nuclear, one- or two-generation household – especially if we also include single-parent and single-person households. However, with an ageing population there are additional complications.[12]

First, the retired themselves constitute a large proportion of such households. Indeed most retired and elderly live in their own home. Much of the care of the elderly, reinforced by the policy of care in the community, is provided through support for those living alone or as aged couples. This becomes increasingly difficult as they advance in years. It has also to be noted that the elderly tend to be among the poorest in society. Many retired persons are living off modest fixed incomes which may be decreasing in value. Many are on state pensions which often do not meet basic needs. They are, therefore, also at a considerable socio-economic disadvantage, having no easy access to transport and being inadequately warmed and fed.

Secondly, the nuclear family is much more mobile, moving to follow work or other demands. This has the effect of loosening the ties of local community and scattering the wider family. Communities where adult children live within a block or two of their parents are few and far between, and becoming rarer. Siblings follow their own separate careers. Middle-class parents, especially, are also more ready to move at retirement, often into a pleasant area as well as smaller premises. There are some areas, notably certain seaside resorts, where the population of the elderly has begun to put strains on the social services. This is another expression of the stratification of urban society and the isolation of particular groups in that society.[13]

It also means that responsibility for caring for elderly parents becomes more difficult. Distances make realistic contact hard to maintain; or one sibling bears the brunt of the responsibility; or they move into one of the children's homes, putting all the responsibility on that particular nuclear family. It is still true that most of the care given to the elderly is done through the family. Nevertheless there is an increasing need, especially for the frail elderly, to be given specialized nursing provision or sheltered accommodation in purpose-run homes. Decisions on these matters are not lightly taken but, inevitably, entry into an old people's home is yet another move which may further weaken contacts with friends, family and neighbours.

There is another change in the pattern of family relationships occasioned by increasing longevity. The normal cycle has moved from three to four generations. So, instead of 45-year-old children looking after 65-year-old parents, there are more 65-year-olds looking after 85-year-olds. Moreover, the new responsibility often comes just at that point when the younger generation themselves become grandparents, having completed their own cycle of bringing up children, managing a career or working to keep the family and pay off the mortgage, and might reasonably expect comparative leisure.

All this has the effect of isolating people from their natural and social links just at the point of vulnerability and failing powers. The process of ageing and approaching death is increasingly divorced from the context of where life has been lived. There is, here, the important concept of 'social death'; that is, a process of detachment from the community which ends up with isolation or effective death, even if the person is still physically alive.[14] It is, at one level, a natural process, for as we get older and powers fail and we withdraw from different activities, our world grows smaller. The classic image is of the elderly person who is now only a spectator but who can still be part of the community by watching, commenting and sometimes manipulating things going on around. But, it can be argued, much in modern society accelerates and accentuates this 'social death' as the elderly are increasingly cut off from family and the neighbourhood. Also, they are encouraged to live, play and socialize together in their own clubs and institutions. This is more strongly seen when living in a home for the elderly. Indeed it is apparent that, even there, a stratification occurs and the active shun the inactive, who are more and more left aside. The final stage is hospitalization, which can last many years and is even more isolating.[15]

Death, in this context, becomes increasingly anonymous. Instead of happening in the midst of daily living, it becomes a special event. A death in the family can happen far away, detached from any part of one's own current family life. To be called to the side of a dying parent often entails breaking up family routine, abandoning work and staying in a strange place. Frequently death has occurred before arriving at the bedside. Funerals also have their artificiality. Wakes and weddings are the only time when the family, or clan, appear together. They meet as strangers not knowing how to react to an event in which they have had little part and with whose rituals they are not familiar. Those who may be caught up in the situation as carers – doctors, clergy, social workers – themselves are at this point marginal, only useful in a formal sense and excluded once death has occurred.

The impression should not be given that the majority of people die forgotten and neglected by family and friends. The fact is that most people adapt well and creatively to changing circumstances and take full advantage of the different opportunities afforded today. The majority of elderly people are very much part of family and community life. However, it is still true to say that certain strong social pressures are observable which people, in their own personal circumstances, have to take into account, accept, counter or manipulate as they can.

4 The public face of death

The effects of the medical and family structures for society's perception of death have to be put into a wider context. The marginalization and privatization of death has also been reflected in and reinforced by contemporary funeral practices. These are inevitably part of an ever-changing pattern, handed down from previous generations, yet also clearly reflecting and reinforcing contemporary perceptions.

The history of the meaning of death and the way the dead are treated, remembered and disposed of is now an important strand of social history. The pioneering work of scholars such as Ariès, whose monumental study took in the sweep of European history, has stimulated further studies and controversies.[16] It is too early to suggest that a broad consensus may be emerging. Rather, the tendency is for more detailed studies to suggest that the whole matter is far more complex than was once assumed, and that generalized statements about past attitudes must be treated with caution. Even so, while recognizing that today, as in the past, there is a real pluriformity in society, it is possible to suggest certain dominant tendencies.

First, most deaths do not occur in the home, though that may be reversing, with more emphasis on care in the community and domiciliary hospice care. But even when death is in the home, the body is seldom (though there are real exceptions: see chapter 6) prepared and laid out in the house. Nor, except in certain more traditional communities, are funerals conducted from the home. The body is normally prepared and laid out at the funeral director's premises, using the chapel of rest. Those who die in institutions are moved to the mortuary and/or funeral parlour as soon as possible, sometimes with odd consequences. Undertakers work in relation to statutory registry areas, and it is not always simple or cheap to transfer the burial to, for example, the deceased's family hometown. The ceremony will therefore normally be held either in a church or at the chapel of rest or in the cemetery church, with (for interments) a committal at the graveside. Indeed, with increasing frequency, there is no religious rite. Specifically non-religious rites are being introduced into what is the last bastion of 'social religion'.[17]

Further, there seems to be a growing tendency to separate the disposal of the body and the commemoration of life. The memorial service has been normal for 'the great and the good'. Now, however, it is not unusual for the burial to be seen as a small, private affair, while inviting the wider circles of friends and colleagues to another occasion. It is also probably true that the traditional wake feast is in decline.

Similarly there is less evidence of communal customs in relation to a death in the neighbourhood. Curtains are not drawn, nor do passers-by pause respectfully. The funeral may draw a crowd for someone reasonably well known in the community, but it is eclectic, drawing people from the various circles with which the deceased was associated, but which may have no other connection than that. Many coming to a funeral may not be known even to the family. Conversely the obsequies for someone who dies away from friends and family can be a very empty and sad affair.

Again mourning rituals have become more and more attenuated. Gone are the elaborate dress and graded restrictions of the Victorian middle and upper classes. It is often claimed that the ritualization of grief is beneficial, but it may also be true that the overemphasis on ritual can inhibit the grief process by its rigidity and the prolonged separation of the bereaved from normal society. Perhaps, however, the contemporary tendency towards casualness and freedom has its own drawbacks. Many, both the bereaved and others, tell of their anxious embarrassment because there is now no framework of etiquette or process of resocialization.[18]

This lack has, to some extent, been filled by the funeral director. Dying and the handling of death have been professionalized. It is the funeral director who controls and conducts the official expression of mourning, offering a complete service, looking after every aspect of the occasion other than the disposal of the will. Indeed there are many different strands that have to be brought together in a normal funeral: from preparing the body and obtaining a death certificate to booking the grave or crematorium, arranging the service and providing transport. This could put considerable strain on the family, especially since there are now seldom those in the community, like those who used to lay out the body, or the parson or family doctor, who can be automatically called in. The modern funeral, however, is a smooth, painless and efficient organization. Stress is, as far as possible, reduced and death made as undisruptive of daily life as possible. The mourners are now clients being taken through a well-rehearsed drama without any embarrassing interruptions.[19]

This tendency to smooth over death is further enhanced by the presentation of the body. Either the body is not seen, being in a coffin, or if the body is laid out for viewing it is made as lifelike as possible. This has, of course, been taken to greater extremes in some American circles.[20]

There is, however, another effect of the funeral package. Its smooth exterior can cover over a number of very real tensions between the medical, legal, religious and personal concerns. This comes to the surface more clearly when, for example, the grief of the family is deepened by the need for a post-mortem; or when the religious customs of the family tradition expect certain rituals to be performed; or when organs are given for transplants.

This last point is of some interest. The advance of medical science has increased the demand for donated organs, and there is considerable social pressure, for example, for people to carry donor cards. Little, however, seems to have been done to explore the psychological and sociological reality that these developments encourage or reflect. For instance, it would seem to reinforce the tendency to assume that the prolongation of life is an unqualified good. At the same time it is discussed in terms of the quality of life enjoyed by the recipients. Gratitude is often expressed for the denoted organ. But what does having a transplant tell us about ourselves as persons? What are the motivations for being willing to give an organ? Is there a new sense (somewhat similar to many early and tribal societies) that human worth and even immortality is found in physical continuity?

Further, burial grounds, especially in urban areas, are detached gardens, often on the edge of the town. The church with its family vaults or familiar churchyard forming part of the living community are seldom any longer used. Increased population and the need for proper health regulations forced changes. But modern graveyards are individualized, personal plots, marked by a carved stone, and often neglected with the passing of time, as families are scattered abroad, or cared for by the local authority. The classic example is Karl Marx's grave in Highgate cemetery. He was buried in a normal grave in a cemetery on the fringe of Victorian London. Only later, when his followers wanted to mark the spot in a suitable way was the grave rescued from obscurity. This is taken a step further by the vast war cemeteries of Europe. Death is even more anonymous and even more entirely individual.

Moreover, the growing tendency to use cremation for the disposal of the body also affects attitudes to death. It underlines the finality of death physically. For those who believe in life after death it suggests a sharper distinction between the body and the soul. Faiths that stress some kind of resurrection tend to resist cremation. Also, with cremation, memorials are less obtrusive or even non-existent. Often a resting place is marked by a tree, or the ashes are scattered in a garden of rest or at a favourite spot at home or in the country. There is a growing movement to link the disposal of the remains with the natural cycle in nature reserves or public gardens.[21]

5   The shadow of death

Perhaps the paradox of our times lies in the contrast between the way death is handled socially and the fact that we live in the most destructive and death-conscious century in history.

It is hard to overestimate the trauma caused by the First World War (1914–18). A whole generation of young men was decimated in the gruesome mudbath of the trenches. Suddenly a civilization, apparently at its peak of cultural, political and economic achievement, was tearing itself apart. War, till then, had been glory on the far-flung boundaries of Empire, part of the price to pay for furthering the cause of civilization. At home prosperity and science were driving away the ravages of poverty, surely if slowly. The years 1914–18 saw a nation caught between the need to see the war as a crusade, guilty and stunned by the wanton destruction and yet needing to salve its national pride. The impact of the experience is witnessed to by the innumerable war memorials and the rituals of Remembrance Day. Yet it also tore a hole in the common assumptions of religious belief and practice and social structures. There was a resolution that it should never happen again.[22]

The shadow of that event is still very much with us, even if it is fading. Nothing since has had such a formative influence on the national psyche – though the 1939–45 war has a similar place in the hearts of Jews and Russians. The Second World War never roused the intensity of anxiety and shock of the first. What has been more important for recent generations has been the threat of nuclear annihilation. The mushroom clouds of Hiroshima and Nagasaki have loomed over the world. For forty years the stand-off between East and West that was the Cold War poised the world above the abyss. In such a situation no one is immune, and there are signs that almost all people were in subtle ways affected. Anxiety can stimulate an active reaction (CND etc.) or be suppressed, enabling people to live 'normal' lives, or be brazened out, accepting the potential use of such weapons.[23]

More recently there has been a further shift. Since the demolition of the Berlin wall a nuclear holocaust may be less of a possibility (but it has not gone away). Instead other forms of mass death have come to the top of the agenda. These have always been there but now are seen in a different framework in a more complicated world. War is still waged, such as the Falklands campaign and Operation Desert Storm; civil wars rumble on in the Balkans and former Soviet Union, south-east Asia and Africa; human and natural disasters cause countless deaths through famine. Signs of hope and peace are constantly overtaken by further tragedy. It is as though the four horsemen of the Apocalypse, war, disease, famine and death, were riding through the world.[24]

Yet the ambiguity remains. It is possible to distance ourselves from all this. In a sense that is inevitable, since in most cases there is little that can be done directly. It is also depersonalized, transmitted through the media, which may of itself add to that indirectness of contact. Over-exposure may even harden the sensibilities. It is, however, surely not possible for death so presented entirely to be set aside. Perhaps we ought to rediscover the virtue of the *memento mori*, to remember that in 'the midst of life we are in death', and to acknowledge more readily our solidarity with others with whom we share life's insecurities and uncertainties.[25]

6   The journey to death

All that has been said so far has been an attempt to suggest some of the issues that help us characterize the perception of death in contemporary society. It would seem that the dominant tendency is not, as Gorer suggests, to suppress a knowledge of death, making it a taboo subject, but of privatizing death. Dying is not part of the community experience but is very much a personal experience. This is a reflection of much of the contemporary lifestyle, in which public and private are clearly separated, and the personal is in the private sector. The natural and proper individual desire to postpone death has also been strengthened by the success of modern medicine and social welfare. It is against this background that people have to begin to face the possibility of their own death. The task in this section is to begin to trace some of the ways in which this is experienced.

For many, death becomes a conscious possibility in having to face the diagnosis of a disease or the acceptance of a condition that cannot be reversed, such as cancer or Aids. Some, of course, will face sudden death, for which there can be no preparation, through accident or other cause. Most, however, will find themselves recognizing that life is moving on and that the future is going to be shorter than the past. It may be at the point of retirement or in the recognition that physical powers are failing. Of course death is the end of every life so, in a real sense, the preparation for death is from birth. But for our purposes attention is directed to the later years, when the thought of death begins to become part of life – from retirement at sixty-five for men (and soon for women), accelerating as one becomes increasingly elderly.

Much has been written about reactions to death and approaching death. Elisabeth Kubler-Ross has been a pioneer in the field and, although her work has been much debated and criticized, she can still provide a basic framework. She offers a five-stage model for the personal journey towards death. It must be emphasized, however, that while such a model suggests a sequence, and there is clearly an experience of process, it cannot be taken as necessary or inevitable. Each person's pilgrimage is unique and may express one or more of the 'stages'. The interest here is to suggest that such a model sets out attitudes that can be widely found in those who, by growing older, are facing death as a factor in daily life. The circumstances of her practice have been in the hospital, working with the terminally ill, where death is imminent. She is also working with a psychological model, and it is in psychology that most work in this area has been done. It is, however, possible to use it effectively in a wider social context, applying it over a longer time scale and as a way to indicate social trends.[26]

The first stage or level is one of denial and shock (characterized as 'Not me?'). This can, in the medical context, include a flat refusal to acknowledge, for example, what has been said by doctors; or the hope that the diagnosis is wrong; or that it will turn out different in this case; or perhaps there will be a miracle cure. This stage, however, can begin a long way back, well before any final diagnosis. In relation to illness it is possible to put off the evil day by denying the symptoms or battling on despite clear problems. Failing powers are not accepted so there is a refusal (e.g.) to use a hearing aid, or to borrow large-print books, or to accept that it is no longer possible to play sport at a certain level.

At the more general level, retirement or a certain birthday, for instance, can make one realize that time is moving on. Yet there is no need to acknowledge the fact while faculties are still reasonably good. Death can be put off for a while yet. There is no virtue in giving in and becoming morbid. Such an attitude is both reasonable and natural. So old age can be a time of adjustment, the opening-up of new opportunities, the discovery of fresh talents and the acquiring of new skills. Advantage can be taken of medical and social aids. The effects of degenerative disease can be countered by surgery or drugs. Despite the gradual closing of the horizons it is still possible to make something of life and to remain positive.[27]

The second stage or level is anger (characterized as 'Why me?'). For those who have been told they have an incurable disease, this is a most natural reaction. It feels as though one has been singled out while others remain free. It is impossible to deny reality, but one feels rejected, discriminated against. God, the world, society, everyone can appear unfair. It does not make sense. The temptation is then to find reasons. 'What have I done to deserve this?' Disease and death have been closely linked with evil and salvation in almost every religion. This is so ingrained that secular people also share the feeling of guilt and disfigurement, of being different, rejected and helpless.

For others, for whom the process is perhaps more drawn out, anger comes out less sharply as a feeling of resentment. There is a kind of banked-up fire smouldering within, which permeates and affects life: resentment at failing powers; of others who can still participate in ways no longer available to us; of those who have certain advantages in health care or better facilities or more caring families. This can be expressed through a dogged determination to carry on, defying the advice of doctors and family to accept growing limitations, or in a soured bitterness that cannot accept reality.

The third level is that of bargaining (characterized by 'Perhaps me – but if I . . .?'). Perhaps it is possible to get out of the bind by striking a bargain. If I take my medicine, keep to my regime, perhaps I can have a reprieve? Or conversely, if certain favours are granted, then in return certain obligations will be undertaken. This, too, is a fundamental human attitude. It has its roots in mutual responsibility and shared living, but it easily becomes a kind of blackmail or abject submission. Religiously it comes out in trying to play games with God, who is obliged to reward good behaviour. It can be seen in those who turn a medical regimen into rigid ritual, offering their actions as a kind of sacrificial liturgy.

The aim could be said to put the brake on the process. By maintaining, for example, regular exercise or keeping to a social routine, shopping, visiting the OAP club, having tea with family or neighbours, there is a sense of achievement and a measured set of demands. Of course there is reason and sense here in sustaining activity and social contacts as long as possible, but there can be a false sense of security, a denial of what is really happening.

These three attitudes are, each in their own way, defiant. The will to life is a strong positive human instinct. Without it there would be no struggle to overcome disability or disaster. The difficulty is to recognize and accept that death is also part of life and shapes and forms our self-understanding. There comes a point when, as it were, there is a necessary change of key, when the shadow of death is accepted into the theme of life. Many may never get to that point, and remain defiant to the end, even to the point of being crushed and destroyed:

> Do not go gentle into that good night,
> Old age should burn and rage at close of day;
> Rage, rage against the dying of the light. (Dylan Thomas)

Others, however, find it possible to move towards death in a more positive way: 'Do not despise death, but be well content with it, since this too is one of those things which nature wills' (M. Aurelius). For most of us, though, this is a hard and difficult transition, not easily or willingly undertaken.[28]

So the fourth stage or level is described as preparatory depression (characterized as 'Right, come on then, its me'). The acceptance of the reality does not necessarily bring peace, but it can bring darkness. Here is a finality that cannot be avoided. All that has made life worthwhile is to be taken away. We are stripped. It is an acceptance of resignation. It is possible to recognize such a disposition quite readily. It can be accompanied by apathy and inertia. Family and friends may be ignored, and necessary tasks seem too much trouble. If there is any mess it can be cleared up by those left behind. Meanwhile it is just as well to wait with a resigned acceptance.

The fifth stage is that of acceptance ('Yes, it is me'). This final stage is positive. Although death is near, or coming over the horizon, it can be received with equanimity if not joy. Meanwhile what time and energies are left can be used creatively. It is possible to enjoy the world, even if only as a spectator, rejoicing in others' successes. Each day is accepted as a gift to be used. Family and friends are welcomed and appreciated; those who care are recognized for all they do; preparations can be made for the end, such as ensuring wills are in order; loose ends can be tied up, reconciliations made, thanks expressed.

Of course, these more positive reactions are not confined to those facing imminent death but can be part of the whole process of moving into old age. The first may result in a kind of uninterested inertia, possibly becoming reclusive. Everything is too much bother. The latter attitude may appear defiant, but may in fact be a new lease of life. If the end is drawing near then everything is precious, to be enjoyed and savoured. It is as though old and familiar things become new, there for the first time, given a new intensity. Yet it is also possible to say farewell without undue anxiety or regret.

This is the sense in which dying is said to be the final stage of growth. Maturity can be defined as living appropriately at any stage of life. So there is a kind of appropriateness in ageing and dying. One can move into the last stage in such a way as to cope with it positively. This is coupled with the sense of readiness to die. There are frequent stories of how people have, perhaps after seeing a child again after many years or after some act of reconciliation, allowed themselves to die. They are willing to let go. The other aspect of this sense of growth is that of rounding off a journey, of finishing a task, of being complete.[29]

Here it is perhaps appropriate to make a number of further points which can help to fill out this outline.

One of the persistent ideas, not least among doctors, is that hope must be sustained. By that is normally meant that a patient has to have some expectation of a positive outcome - i.e. cure or remission. Sometimes that is sustained by suppressing information or not admitting to a bad prognosis. There is considerable discussion of the desirability of such a policy, not least because if false hope is held out and it fails, it can lead to even greater disappointment. In any case the patient can often tell what is not being said, and such a policy merely results in a conspiracy of silence. Not to face the truth can often foreclose a proper grieving process for both patient and family. Increasingly it is being seen that, with sensitivity and skill, recognizing the possibility of exceptional cases when perhaps the patient is not ready to listen to the truth, it is better that the situation is open between all concerned.

Part of the problem, however, has been the inability to recognize different kinds of hope. It is not wrong to hope for cure or respite, but there are other realistic forms of hope that can accept the prospect of death yet put it into some kind of proportion. The obvious form of such hope is life after death. But there are also hopes for children, for spouse, for the continuity of a life's work. Hope does not mean betting against the odds or indulging in wishful thinking, but an acceptance of reality in a positive and creative way that affirms the future even in the midst of death. There can be false (even false religious) hopes and healthy (even healthy religious) hopes. Pastoral care, in conjunction with medical care where appropriate, will try to enable people to keep hope, but a positive, realistic hope.[30]

This leads to a consideration of how important a faith or a metaphysic is for those approaching death. There is evidence to suggest that those who have a mature working faith structure, whether religious or not, can adjust more easily to the nearness of death than those who do not. A mature faith or world view is one that provides both a reasoned and satisfying perspective on life and can take into account life's challenges, experiences and discontinuities. It does not have to be able to provide an answer for all circumstances but can sustain one through 'the valley of the shadow' as well as at more serene moments. On the other hand, a too rigid or simplistic set of beliefs is often too brittle to withstand the impact of life's ills, and a merely inherited or conventional faith system will not be deeply rooted enough to sustain itself under pressure. This means that there can be more or less adequate forms of religious or non-religious beliefs. This quality of faith is closely bound to the person's life story as it has built their character over the years. In other words, it is not only the truth and adequacies of the beliefs themselves but also the formation of the personality through and around them that enables a person to handle the reality of death.[31]

It is also of interest to ask what is thought of as a 'good death'. In a former age, to die a good death would have been to have made proper preparation, to have gathered the family round so that one could say farewell and be seen to be at peace. Last words were important as indicating the state of the soul at the solemn moment. To some extent this has been recovered by the hospice movement, with its emphasis on approaching death with dignity. However, each week in the *Guardian* a personality, in responding to a series of questions, is asked how they would want to die. In line with our suggestion that death is essentially understood as a private, individual event to be minimized in importance, almost without exception the reply is to slip quietly away in sleep. The emphasis is on lack of fuss, little warning and no pain. It also suggests that there has been a shift in interest from the point of death towards the process of dying. Time and again one hears that being dead, death itself, does not carry any anxiety, but there are considerable qualms about the manner of dying. There is a desire not to die helpless and after a long period of atrophy, nor to die in pain.[32]

Death, of course, is always unpredictable and difficult. However well prepared, no one is without some fear at the door of death; no one is spared the shock of bereavement. And death, however careful we are of the dignity of the one dying, is usually a messy, agonizing and tortuous experience for both the one dying and for those around. It is wrong to sentimentalize or romanticize. Whatever we may want to say about death, it comes to each person differently and we all react differently. Ideals must not impose expectations. People must be allowed to be themselves and to live out their own experience. The task of the counsellor is to provide support and stability as a companion on another's journey so that they can make the best of themselves and their circumstances.

7   Conclusion

This chapter has tried to look at the way society handles the problem of mortality. We have looked at how people experience the process of dying and how society as a whole expresses its perception of death. At this point, however, it must be stressed that generalizations must be tempered with two cautions. First, as has been noted from time to time, no two deaths are the same. We each have to walk our own path from life into death. Secondly, and more importantly, we have to take into account the pluralism of our society. There are, of course, variations of perspective and practice according to locality and generation. Some communities continue to reflect earlier cultural patterns. But in recent decades Britain has also become more ethnically, religiously and culturally diverse. This is not least expressed in the customs and rituals that surround the central mystery of human existence. The association of death and dying with the private sphere makes it possible for these variations to exist side by side, both within Christianity and between such religious groups as Hindu, Muslim or Buddhist (see chapter 6 for further discussion).[33]

The sociological perspective that this chapter has attempted to address is important on a number of accounts. First, it provides the context within which we each have to make sense of our own dying and within which those engaged in caring for the dying have to work. Secondly, it provides a context for the ethical debates

about death and dying that face us today. Ethical issues are never
faced in a vacuum but reflect the contemporary context. How a
society deals with the reality of death embodies our deepest beliefs
about the nature and worth of humanity. This is the heart of moral
choice. Thirdly, those who are engaged in the care of the dying also
have to take cognizance of those social and psychological realities
that shape our self-understanding. Both social policy and pastoral
care deal with questions of personal dignity and ask how our life
together should be shaped in order to express what it means to live
and die as human beings.

Notes

1   In G. Gorer, 'The pornography of death', *Encounter* (October 1955);
    see also his *Death, Grief and Mourning* (London, Cresset, 1965).
2   Taken from Clive Seale, 'Demographic change and the care of the
    dying 1969–87', in Donna Dickenson and Malcolm Johnson, *Death,
    Dying and Bereavement* (London, Sage, 1983), 55ff. For further infor-
    mation see, e.g., OPCS, *Mortality Statistics: England and Wales 1987:
    Canoe* (London, HMSO, 1989) and other analyses of official statistics.
3   See David Cannadine, 'War and death, grief and mourning in modern
    Britain', in Joachim Whaley, *Mirrors of Mortality* (London, Europa,
    1981).
4   For reactions to retirement see, e.g., Rory Williams, *A Protestant
    Legacy* (Oxford, Clarendon, 1990). esp. I.2; also Paul H. Ballard, *In
    and Out of Work* (Edinburgh, St Andrews, 1990).
5   See Philip A. Mellor, 'Death in high modernity', in D. Clark, *The
    Sociology of Death* (Oxford, Blackwell, 1993). (The volume also
    includes a useful summary of the present sociological discussion by
    Tony Walter.) See also Michael Butler and Ann Orbach, *Being Your Age*
    (London, SPCK, 1993).
6   Langdon Gilkey, *Religion and the Scientific Future* (London, SCM,
    1970). For discussions of the doctors' dilemma, see relevant contribu-
    tions to Dickenson and Johnson, op. cit.
7   R. A. Lambourne, 'Towards an understanding of medical theological
    dialogue', in Michael Wilson, *Explorations in Health and Salvation*
    (Birmingham, Institute for the Study of Worships and Religious
    Architecture, 1983), which includes the 'Concepts map for the prac-
    tice of medicine', p.223. See also Michael Wilson, *Health is for People*
    (London, Darton, Longman and Todd, 1975).
8   See, e.g. Sandd Stoddard, *The Hospice Movement: A Better Way to Care*

for the Dying (London, Cape, 1978).

9   Bruce D. Rumbold, *Helplessness and Hope* (London, SCM, 1986), ch.
    1.

10 Ibid.

11 Paul H. Ballard, 'The social context of the family today', *Contact*, 114
    (1994).

12 See Seale, op. cit.

13 See e.g. Daniel Ley, *A Social Geography of the City* (New York, Harper
    and Row, 1983), ch. 3.

14 Michael Mulkay, 'Social death in Britain', in D. Clark, op. cit. Eleanor
    D. Gatliffe, *Death in the Classroom* (London, Epworth, 1988) offers a
    way to counteract this through a course for schools.

15 See e.g. Elizabeth Dean, 'Sitting it out', in Dickenson and Johnson,
    op. cit., and Butler and Orbach, op. cit.

16 Phillipe Ariès, *The Hour of Our Death* (London, Allen Lane, 1981).
    See also e.g, Joachim Whaley, op. cit. and specialist studies, D. Clark,
    Between Pulpit and Pew (Cambridge, CUP, 1982); Rory Williams, op.
    cit.; Rosemary Paine, 'Death in Ireland', in Dickenson and Johnson
    op. cit.

17 See, for the general development, Michael Young, 'Right choice for
    rites of passage', *The Guardian*, 23 July 1994.

18 See Williams, op. cit., ch. 4; also Cannadine, op. cit. For a survey of
    Australian attitudes and practices see Graeme M. Griffin and Des
    Tobin, *In the Midst of Life . . .* (Melbourne, University Press, 1982).

19 Glennys Howarth, 'Investigating death-work', in D. Clark, op. cit.
    (193); also Griffin and Tobin, op. cit.

20 The classic account is Jessica Mitford, *The American Way of Death*
    (London, Hutchinson, 1963); but see also the report on being buried
    near your hero in *The Guardian*, 15 August 1994.

21 See report in *The Guardian*, 23 July 1994; also Williams, op. cit.: Peter
    Jupp, 'Cremation or burial', in D. Clark, op. cit. (1990).

22 See David Cannadine, op. cit.

23 Ibid.

24 Revelation 6:1–8.

25 Such reminders are traditionally to be found, e.g. on memorials in
    churches, especially in some medieval tombs where a skeleton is
    carved alongside the effigy, or in paintings and portraits in the
    Renaissance period. Quotation from *Book of Common Prayer* (1662).

26 Elisabeth Kubler-Ross, *Death, the Final Stage of Growth* (Englewood
    Cliffs, Prentice Hall, 1975); *Living with Death and Dying* (London,
    Souvenir, 1981).

27 See Williams, op. cit., ch. 2. Also Ian Ainsworth-Smith and Peter
    Speck, *Letting Go* (London, SPCK, 1982).

28   See also Sheila Cassidy, *Light from the Dark Valley* (London, Darton Longman and Todd, 1994); and Dickenson and Johnson, op. cit., part 4.

29   See Elisabeth Kubler-Ross, op. cit. (1975), chs. 5 and 6. For a summary of a number of maturational theories see Michael Jacobs, *Towards the Fullness of Christ* (London, Darton, Longman and Todd, 1988). There are a number of personal stories, e.g. in Dickenson and Johnson, op. cit.; Mary Austin, *Free to Dance with the Lord of the Dance* (London, Epworth, 1992); Jo Ann Kelley Smith, *Free Fall* (London, SPCK, 1975).

30   Rumbold, op. cit., ch. 4.

31   Graeme M. Griffin, *Death and the Church* (Melbourne, Dove, 1978), 64ff; Williams, op. cit., ch. 9.

32   Mary Bradbury, 'Contemporary representations of "good" and "bad" death', in Dickenson and Johnson, op. cit. For a theological/pastoral reflection, see Henri M. Nouwen, *Our Greatest Gift* (London, Hodder and Stoughton, 1994).

33   Williams, op. cit., ch. 9. For a broad interfaith survey, see John Bowker, *The Meanings of Death* (Cambridge, CUP, 1991). Also, for greater detail: Donald P. Irish et al., *Ethnic Variations in Dying, Death, and Grief* (Washington, Taylor and Francis, 1993); G. R. Dunstan and Mary Sellers, *Consent in Medicine* (London, King's Fund, 1983); Arthur Berger et al., *Perspectives on Death and Dying* (Philadelphia, Charles, 1989).

3
Measuring the quality of life

ANDREW EDGAR

1 Introduction

The attempt to measure 'quality of life' has been a concern of
social scientists for some time. The 1970s and 1980s saw a rapid
expansion in the number of these means, and a development in
their sophistication, in the fields of health economics and
epidemiology[1]. The motivations behind this research are various.
At base it is recognized that the improvement of the quality of
life of a patient is either one of the objectives of health care
(alongside disease prevention, alleviation of symptoms and pain,
provision of humane care and prolongation of life), or is synony-
mous with the improvement of health itself. As such,
measurement of changes in patients' quality of life is indicative
of the achievements of a health service. As chronic and disabling
diseases become more prevalent, measures of achievement that
are more subtle than crude mortality rates or years of patient
survival become increasingly important. Quality of life may
therefore be invoked as part of a medical audit, and may thus
serve a role in demonstrating the efficiency and effectiveness of
any medical interventions or services, and such quality-of-life
measures may be used in the assessment of new medical technology. Broadly based measuring instruments, such as the
Sickness Impact Profile (which takes account of patients'
emotional behaviour, their ability to work and to manage their
homes, and to enjoy recreational and social activities), may
further be used as a routine complement to existing, typically
biological or physiological, measures of a patient's health status,
in order to record changes in the patient's behaviour and subjective reactions to his or her health, or to indicate the relationship

between social or environmental factors and health. Through a comparison of quality of life (as the output of medical care) and the costs of the care, indications can be taken of the cost-efficiency of a treatment. Most controversially, quality-of-life measures may be employed to guide the allocation of scarce health-care resources (between specialisms, forms of treatment, or even between patients), in response to the pressure exerted by the increasing expense of health-care interventions and an increase in the demand for medical treatment. The range of measures of quality of life that have been, and continue to be, developed is largely explained by the need to tailor measures for specific purposes.

Two uses of quality-of-life measures involving decisions about the life and death of patients may be distinguished. On the one hand, as an instrument for the allocation of scarce resources, quality-of-life measures may appear to justify a withdrawal of resources from a medical specialism, or from certain categories of patient. It may be argued that greater benefits will be achieved if a given sum of money is used to carry out, for example, a dozen hip replacements rather than a single heart transplant, or that patients with lung diseases are unlikely to improve suffi-ciently to justify their receipt of a coronary by-pass operation. Patients thereby deprived of treatment face premature death. On the other hand, a specific patient may be deemed to have a quality of life that is so low that its maintenance is undesirable, and thus that death is preferable to the patient's current quality of life.

In this chapter, I will illustrate the development, design and application of quality-of-life measures through reference to the Quality Adjusted Life Year (QALY). I will rehearse a defence of the QALY approach that sees it as a potential indicator of the public's pre-existing attitudes to and opinions on health-care resource allocation. I will suggest that, if this is a fair defence (and this is a big 'if'), then QALYs might indicate a society's collective opinion as to the limits of a worthwhile life (and thus upon the health conditions that would justify allowing a patient to die). I will then examine the ways in which quality-of-life measures may be implicated in life-and-death decisions about patients, specifically by exploring the understanding of death that is implicit in these measures. It will be concluded that current formulations of quality-of-life measures are based upon too narrow an understanding of death, and indeed of life itself, insofar as they fail to recognize the need for the cultural resources that are necessary to make sense of (especially premature) death.

2 QALYs

The fundamental idea that grounds the Quality Adjusted Life Year involves the assumption that a year of good health can be given the value 1. A year of unhealthy life has a value of less than 1, with death being given the value 0. From this initial assumption, the construction of the quality-of-life measure proceeds through the definition of a series of health states. Each state is then given an appropriate value or weight. Rosser and Kind initially defined health states in terms of only two parameters: objective disability and subjective distress. Disability was subdivided into eight degrees, and distress was subdivided into four degrees.[2] (The categories are listed in table 1.)

This served to define thirty-two states, of which three were omitted (as it was argued that distress is irrelevant to someone who is unconscious). The values to be attributed to each state were ascertained through interviews with seventy subjects. (This group was composed of medical patients, psychiatric in-patients, general and psychiatric nurses, doctors and healthy volunteers. It must be stressed that, although the original QALY valuations have tended to be taken as definitive, this was very much a pilot study.) The interview began with the request to order six 'marker states' according to their relative severity, and then, for the purpose of placing these states on a scale, the ordered marker states were taken in pairs, with the interviewee being asked to say 'how many times more ill is a person described as being in state 2 as compared with state 1?' Interviewees were asked to determine the ratio through reflection on the proportion of resources that they considered it justifiable to allocate between the two states, and as an expression of the interviewee's 'point of indifference between curing one of the iller people or a number (specified by the ratio) of the less ill people'. The remaining twenty-three health states were then subjected to a similar treatment. The interviewees were also asked to place death somewhere on their scale.[3]

Table 1   Classification of states of sickness

Disability

1. No disability.

2. Slight social disability

3. Severe disability and/or slight impairment of performance at work. Able to do all housework except very heavy tasks.

4. Choice of work or performance at work very severely limited. Housewives and old people able to do light housework only but to go out shopping.

5. Unable to undertake any paid employment. Unable to continue any education. Old people confined to home except for escorted outings and unable to do shopping. Housewives able only to perform a few simple tasks.

6. Confined to chair or to wheelchair or able to move around in the home only with support from an assistant.

7. Confined to bed.

8. Unconscious.

A. No distress.

B. Mild distress (slight pain which is relieved by aspirin).

C. Moderate distress (pain which is not relieved by aspirin).

D. Severe distress (pain for which heroin is prescribed).

Source: Rosser and Kind, 1978, 349

The QALY matrix is not disease-specific, which is to say that, in principle, a patient suffering from any disease, and at any point in the development of that disease, can position her current experience of the disease on the matrix. Given appropriate statistical information on the prognoses of patients with or without treatment, or undergoing alternative treatments, the QALY matrix can be used to assess the changes to a patient's quality of life that result from treatment.

For example, a patient who, without treatment, would continue to live for a further twenty years in state 4A (and thus limited in the type of work he or she can undertake, but suffering no distress) would enjoy 19·28 QALYs. If it is assumed that treatment A will facilitate a complete cure and add a further ten years to the patient's life, then a further 10·72 QALYs would be yielded, or the equivalent of an extra 10·72 years of good health. If we assume that an alternative treatment (B) would give the

Table 2   QALY (matrix marker states in italics)

Disability	A	B	C	D
		Distress		
1	1.000	0.995	*0.990*	0.967
2	0.990	0.986	0.973	*0.932*
3	0.980	0.972	0.956	0.912
4	0.964	0.956	0.942	0.870
5	0.946	*0.935*	0.900	0.700
6	0.875	*0.845*	0.680	0.000
7	0.677	0.564	0.000	*−1.486*
8	−1.028	−	−	−

Source: Kind, Rosser and Williams, 1982, 160.

patient thirty-five years of life, but with slight (rather than no) disability (and thus a health state of 2A), the QALY approach can be used to assist in deciding which treatment to use. (It may be noted that an appeal to mere longevity would immediately favour B.) By the QALY calculation, B yields an extra 15.37 years of healthy life, in comparison to no treatment at all (i.e. 34.65–19.28). In comparison to treatment A, B offers the patient an extra 4.65 QALYs. B thus remains the favoured treatment. B's superiority is only challenged when its cost is taken into account. If we assume that treatment A costs £10,000, then each extra QALY it yields comes at the cost of £932.84 (i.e. 10,000/10.72). If B costs £15,000, then each extra QALY costs £975.93 (i.e. 15,000/15.37). Thus, while B may give the patient a longer life, and the equivalent of more years of good health, it is the less cost-efficient treatment. If there were only £30,000 available to treat this particular disease, the use of treatment A would not simply allow the treatment of more patients (three as to two treatments of B), but would also yield 32.16 QALYs, as opposed to only 30.74 QALYs yielded by spending £30,000 on treatment B. (It may be noted that although an extra patient is being treated, the other two are being condemned to die five years earlier than is technically necessary.)

The QALY is an example of a health status index. Indexes facilitate the comparison of diverse health states, and thus allocation decisions. The health of the patient is expressed as a single value, however many aspects (or 'parameters') of the health states are taken into account. It may be noted that indexes can be compiled using more than two parameters. For example, EuroQol is a more sophisticated form of the QALY. The two dimensions of distress and disability are replaced by the six dimensions of mobility, self-care, activity (such as work, housework and study), social relationships, pain and mood. Interviewees are asked to rank descriptions of health states that specify the condition of each of these six dimensions.[4]

An alternative approach to the measurement of health states does not seek to reduce the diverse parameters to a single value. Instead, a 'profile' is provided, that maps the patient's performance on each parameter separately. A particular combination of performances is not necessarily judged to be an improvement over an alternative combination. Such measures will be of use in assessing a patient's progress, or in assessing the efficacy of medical interventions. Profiles typically allow a more comprehensive and subtle account of a health state (albeit an increase in dimensions leads to a corresponding increase in the complexity of the task of eliciting appropriate responses from patients), and may readily be tailored to be receptive to particular diseases.[5]

3   A defence of QALYs

The use of QALYs, particularly in the allocation of health-care resources, is typically defended on the grounds that they allow us to calculate the most efficient use of scarce health-care resources and thereby maximize the amount of good health that can be generated.[6] Paul T. Menzel has, however, proposed a distinctive defence of QALYs.[7] Menzel's argument rests on the use that quality-of-life measures make of survey data. His suggestion is that it is possible so to construct the quality-of-life questionnaire that the QALY matrix comes to represent the population's 'prior consent' to specific allocations of health care resources. In effect, the questionnaire is seen to sample, and indeed focus, public opinion about allocation, thereby giving legitimacy to the allocation decisions made upon the basis of the QALY matrix. Menzel begins by noting that QALYs rest on the intuition that, all other things being equal, I would prefer a shorter life of good health than a longer life of poor health. The exact figures that I would give to the length of these respective lives and the degree of poor health suffered are indicative of the QALY weightings I would affirm. (A standard form of enquiry in quality of life surveys is the 'time trade-off'. The respondent is asked how much shorter a life in good health he or she would find preferable to a longer lifetime with a given disability and/or distress.) However, to say that I would be happy with my lot should I die prematurely having avoided moderate disability, is not to say that I would be happy if my long disabled life was to be allowed to end prematurely in order to preserve the short healthy life of another. That is to say that a choice between two possibilities for my life does not entail the affirmation of a choice between my life and that of another. This is indeed the crux of John Harris's now famous criticism of QALYs. To choose between two lives, or more significantly, to allow one person to live for, say, an extra seven years of good health, while depriving five others of the possibility of an extra one year each, overlooks the fact that each person involved wants to live equally fervently. Harris therefore prefers to allocate resources according to the number of lives saved, noting that a 'disaster is the greater the more victims there are, the more lives that are lost', no matter how long, or how good, each life is.[8] Menzel's response may be seen to rest upon the assumption that justice entails the need for individuals within a society to make sacrifices for each other. Given scarce medical resources, the extreme sacrifice is for me to be prepared to give up my minimal (albeit, to me, precious) life expectancy, for another.

Menzel suggests that QALY respondents should be presented with questions that explicate the life-and-death implications of their expressed preferences. He therefore proposes a 'QALY bargain', by which the respondent specifies the degree of risk that he or she is willing to take of being allowed to die due to a poor QALY prognosis, in return for the increased chance of being saved if he or she has a good QALY prognosis. In effect, Menzel is arguing that, if we are divorced from our personal interest in our continued well-being, and thus from the psychological fact that we may all want to go on living equally fervently, we could endorse a particular, unequal and yet non-arbitrary allocation of scarce health-care resources as being rationally justifiable on grounds akin to those explicated by the QALY concept. The consequence of this endorsement is that, should a catastrophe befall me and I am left with the prospect of a very low quality-of-life, then I accept that I am of lower priority in the queue for health-care resources than someone with good prospects, even if that entails my death.

Two reservations may be noted concerning Menzel's argument. Firstly, it is not clear that any complex modern society would give rise to a consensus on health care allocation, even if confronted by the QALY bargain. It is notable that Rosser and Kind, in researching their original QALY matrix, also produced matrices for each of the six subgroups that made up their sample population. Each group generated a distinctive matrix. This suggests that any individual is unlikely to have actually consented to the matrix of the aggregate population, and thus that his or her response to the QALY bargain is unlikely to be respected in practice. Secondly, in that the QALY bargain works by eliciting existing public opinion, it entails that any allocation based upon the bargain will be legitimate only relative to that public. It has been suggested by a number of commentators that the existing dependence of QALYs on surveys of the general public is liable to expose subsequent allocation decisions to that population's prejudices and biases. For example, a population that is, in general, highly intolerant of the severely disabled may skew the weighting of the matrix significantly against that group, thereby depriving them of health-care resources.[9] While the separation of the QALY matrix from reference to any specific diseases and health condition mitigates the danger, it remains conceivable that the QALY bargain might reflect our fear at being condemned to live amongst a stigmatized social group, rather than our simple reaction to the prospect of disability and distress. These points will be seen to colour the following discussion.

4 Death

We may now turn to the possibility of using quality-of-life measures as a guide or justification for decisions about the removal of health care from, or even the active euthanasia of, certain individuals. It may be noted that the QALY matrix allows a negative weighting for certain health states. In Rosser and Kind's original matrix, the conditions of being confined to bed in moderate pain (C7), and confined to a wheelchair in severe pain

(D6) are both judged as being equivalent to death. Unconsciousness (A8) and confinement to bed in severe distress (D7) both received negative weights, and thus are considered to be worse than death. While advocates of quality-of-life measures warn that 'physicians must resist use of . . . measures to justify withholding resources from patients with low ratings',[10] negative weightings might be taken to entail that it is in the interests of a patient who chronically suffers under such conditions to be allowed to die. In effect, euthanasia would yield more QALYs than any life-sustaining treatment. (Other indexes, including EuroQol and the Index of Well-Being, also allow for this possibility.) Given its grounding in survey material, it may be suggested that, at least in principle, the QALY matrix represents a collective view on the limits of a bearable life.

William Aiken refers to the use of the concept of quality of life to justify the removal of resources from particular individuals as its 'exclusionary' use.[11] At its worst it entails that any individual who does not achieve a given quality of life, for whatever reason, should be deprived of the resources necessary to continue that life. Aiken is critical of such arguments on the grounds that they presuppose that any person who cannot strive towards an ideal life, or even what most people would regard as a normal life, has a life of no value whatsoever. This is clearly an extreme assumption. The fact that an individual is currently unable to aspire to an ideal quality of life is not a ground to devalue his life altogether (and so deny him necessary resources). It may rather give grounds for providing him with such resources as will allow him to prosper. This approach becomes problematic when the individuals concerned are incapable of so benefiting, and when their current quality of life does not even attain to the human minimum. Aiken gives the examples of the irreversibly comatose and 'severely defective newborns'. Aiken suggests that in such cases we are prepared to consider allowing the individuals to die, but only because there are costs entailed in keeping them alive. His comment that these individuals are perceived to be consuming '[v]aluable resources which could better be used to enhance the quality of of the lives of others' (p. 32) is coherent with the use of QALYs. Similar resources would be better used, a QALY-based recommendation could read, in improving the quality of life of a patient capable of conscious and purposeful action, rather than in maintaining an individual in an irreversible coma. While Aiken seemingly accepts this line of argument, he is at pains to point out that the removal of resources from the individual does not thereby exclude her from moral consideration. The person remains worthy of respect, and may not thus be abused (for example, as the victim of experimentation). It may be added that, according to the QALY way of thinking, it is in the interests of those with a permanent negative quality of life to die. Death would alleviate an excessively burdensome existence. Allowing her death is thereby an act respectful of certain moral interests of the individual.

Aiken is not, however, concerned exclusively with the economic costs of keeping an individual alive. He refers to the 'financial, resource allocational, or emotional' costs (p. 32). His reference to emotional costs is significant. It opens up speculation as to what is entailed in a worthless life, and more precisely of who bears the costs of such a life. I will argue that it is the costs borne by the patient, in the form of indignity or the continuation of a meaningless life, that are most significant. Aiken's argument, and more importantly the QALY approach, tend to focus on the costs borne by others.

Emotional costs may be borne by the relatives, close friends or carers of the patient. This would be particularly the case in Aiken's two examples of life lived beneath the human minimum. Both cases would fall under A8 (and thus have a value of -1.028) in the QALY matrix, and thus be adjudged worse than death. This is revealing. If it is accepted that permanent unconsciousness is the absence of experience, and thus presumably akin to death, then it may be suggested that A8 deserves a score of zero, or only marginally less than zero. The marked negative weighting seemingly reflects either respondents' anticipation of their own potential permanent unconsciousness, or their distress at seeing others in that state. In the second case, the judgement is that of an observer, rather than someone who experiences the state. The QALY may thereby privilege the emotional costs borne by observers, rather than those borne by the patient. QALY weightings in general appear to reflect our distress at the indignity suffered by another, or our fearful anticipation of falling into such undignified states. As such, it may be suggested, they go beyond mere health-related quality-of-life, to a normative judgement as to what it is to be human. (The danger of irrational prejudice influencing the QALY score may be recalled.) Aiken's concern over the exclusionary use of quality-of-life criteria is thereby affirmed, insofar as QALYs may grossly undervalue states that deviate significantly from some perceived norm of human existence.

An alternative interpretation of emotional cost is as the cost of adjusting to the severely disabling condition. Brock cites the main character of the play *Whose Life is it Anyway?*, asserting that she 'does not want to become the kind of person who is happy in that debilitated and dependent state'.[12] His point is not that this is the inevitable or universal reaction to the possibility of severe disability, but rather that it is one possibility that highlights the resources that the patient requires in order to come to terms with disability. More precisely, it serves to reveal the role that (good) health plays as a precondition of our own conduct of a normal, dignified and, above all, meaningful life. The continuation of a normal life in the absence of good health requires alternative resources. These resources may take the form of medical technology and care, and the emotional and cultural resources necessary to reconsider what is possible and what is worth doing. In this light, the life no longer worth living is that in which no such resources are available to the patient, or no such resources can be utilized by the patient.

This line of inquiry may be developed through a more detailed reflection on the concepts of 'life' and 'health'. Brock draws on the distinction between a 'biological life' and a 'biographical life'. His point is that a person's life is not worth preserving unless that person has the capacity to give meaning to his life. The meaningful or biographical life is 'lived from the "inside"'. It is characterized by the person's 'capacity to form desires, hopes, and plans for the future'. It is '"life" understood as a connected plan or unfolding biography with a beginning, middle, and end' (p. 116). Quality-of-life measures are relevant to this conception insofar as they highlight the health-related preconditions of a biographical life. Health, broadly defined so that it embraces social and environmental factors, is treated as a means to the end of a meaningful life. As Brock notes, quality-of-life measures typically focus on the patient's dysfunctions or, in McEwen's defence of the Nottingham Health Profile (NHP), the patient's need for health care, where need is to be understood in terms of the discrepancy of the measured health state from some more or less well defined norm of good health.[13] As such, quality-of-life measures reflect the conditions to which health-care resources must be directed in order to maintain the possibility of the patient leading a normal (and thus meaningful) life.

While the provision of normal health may indeed facilitate a meaningful life, it cannot be argued that the absence of normal (or good) health necessarily entails a meaningless or worthless life. To make this equation is to fall into the trap, identified by Aiken, of only considering the ideal life as worthwhile. It may also be suggested that it is the trap into which the main character of *Whose Life is it Anyway?* falls. As Brock is at pains to point out, the effect of disability (or dysfunction) on a person's life will vary, depending on the goals she has in life, and her flexibility in reinterpreting and modifying those goals (p. 123). More precisely, the disability may itself be seen as posing a challenge that gives new meaning to one's life. Kagawa-Singer's study of the different ways in which Anglo-Americans and Japanese-Americans cope with terminal cancer is illuminating. She notes that these 'individuals used a definition of health which was based upon their ability to maintain a sense of integrity as productive, able and valued individuals within their social spheres, despite their physical condition.' A woman with metastatic cancer is thus able to declare that 'I am really very healthy. I just have this problem, but I am still me'.[14] Kagawa-Singer concludes that, while individuals drew on the different resources provided for them by their (Japanese or Anglo-American) cultures, they all tended to measure their self-worth, and thus the degree to which their lives remained meaningful, by their ability to fulfil social roles, in spite of their illnesses (p. 303).

It is notable that Kagawa-Singer's subjects did not find the imminence of death, and thus the finitude of their remaining lives, disruptive of their sense of living a meaningful life. Faced with a finite future, patients reassessed the priorities in their lives, so that long-term and abstract objectives were replaced by short-term and concrete goals, such as the enjoyment of family life. This contrasts with John Harris's assertions that the imminence of death merely discolours life, leaving it 'joyless', and that only the open-endedness of life makes it worth living. He concludes that if 'life had a short and finite (rather than indefinite) future, most things would not seem to be worth doing and the whole sense of the worth of life as an enterprise would evaporate'.[15] These assertions rest uneasily with his defence of the preservation of life (providing that the patient wants to live), even if that life is of minimal quality. It may be suggested that Harris here remains insensitive to the subtlety of the concept of biographical life. From his perspective, death can only be presented as the forestalling and disruption of a meaningful life. Death itself is meaningless and undignified. Death thereby becomes something to be feared, and thus permanently deferred. The transformation of a fervent wish to live into a fervent wish not to die suggests a failure to reflect upon the cultural resources that are available to individuals to allow them to make sense of premature death. The initial intuitive attraction of Harris's argument may well rest upon the fact that healthy people are routinely unaware of such resources.

In the light of a similar discussion, Brock indicates the importance of the inclusion within quality-of-life measures of some indication of the patient's response to his or her illness (and specifically, it may be added, to chronic or terminal illness). The Quality of Life Index considers the patient's 'outlook', and the Sickness Impact Profile, a little less specifically, records 'emotional behaviour'. The Nottingham Health Profile similarly contains statements relating to emotional reactions and social isolation. It may however be stressed that the mere recognition of such parameters is of less significance than the importance they are given, and the way in which that importance is derived and statistically recorded (or weighted). Again, if this weighting depends upon the surveying of the general population, and that population lacks the resources to cope meaningfully with terminal illness and death, the weighting may distort the actual experience of illness, and thus the worth of life lived in the face of terminal illness.

5 Conclusion

While the original QALY matrix does not obviously record the patient's response to illness in terms of meaning (except insofar as it is swept up in subjective distress), the weighting of states as worse than death is significant. While in general it cannot be denied that being confined to bed in severe pain is undesirable, it is not inconceivable that certain individuals will have the personal and cultural resources necessary to cope, and give meaning and dignity to this condition. This is, in effect, to repeat the initial criticism of Menzel. The interpretation of QALYs as the reflection of a public consensus on the minimal conditions of a worthwhile life tends to leave the exceptional individual vulnerable. Further, it is to suggest that a negative weighting does not merely indicate a worthless life, but rather the need for cultural as well as medical resources to restore meaning to such life. There will, inevitably, be health states in which the patient cannot benefit from such resources, which is to say, where the emotional costs of a low quality of life are excessive for the patient him- or herself. A quality-of-life measure that is sensitive to the centrality of biographical life may facilitate the recognition of such conditions.

Notes

[1] Richard G. Brooks, *Health Status and Quality of Life Measurement* (Lund, Swedish Institute for Health Economics, 1991).
[2] Rachel Rosser and Paul Kind, 'A scale of valuations of states of illness: is there a social consensus?', *International Journal of Epidemiology*, 7 (4) (1978), 347–58.
[3] Paul Kind, Rachel Rosser and Alan Williams, 'Valuation of Quality of Life: some psychometric evidence', in M. W. Jones-Lee (ed.), *The Value of Life and Safety* (Leiden, North Holland Publishing, 1982), 159–70.
[4] The EuroQol Group, 'EuroQol – a new facility for the measurement of health-related quality of life', *Health Policy*, 16 (1990), 199–208.
[5] M. S. Salek, 'Measuring the quality of life of patients with skin disease', in Stuart R. Walker and Rachel M. Rosser (eds.), *Quality of Life Assessment: Key Issues in the 1990s* (Dordrecht, Boston and London, Kluwer, 1993) 355–70.
[6] Alan Williams, *Economics, QALYs and Medical Ethics: A Health Economist's Perspective* (York Centre for Health Economics, 1994).
[7] Paul T. Menzel, *Strong Medicine: The Ethical Rationing of Health Care* (New York and Oxford, Oxford University Press, 1990).

8   John Harris, 'QALYfying the value of life', *Journal of Medical Ethics*, 13 (1987), 117–23.
9   Roger Crisp, 'Deciding who will die: QALYs and political theory', *Politics*, 9 (1) (1989), 31–5; David Lamb, 'Priorities in health care: reply to Lewis and Charney', *Journal of Medical Ethics*, 15 (1989), 33–4.
10 C. F. McCartney and D. B. Larson, 'Quality of life in patients with gynecologic cancer', *Cancer*, 60 (Suppl.) (1987), 2, 129–36, cited in Brooks, *Health Status*, 10.
11 William Aiken, 'The quality of life', *Applied Philosophy*, 1 (1982), 26–36, at 30–3.
12 Dan Brock, 'Quality of life measures in health care and medical ethics', in Martha Nussbaum and Amartya Sen (eds.), *The Quality of Life* (Oxford, Clarendon Press, 1993), 95–132, at 123.
13 James McEwen, 'The Nottinghamshire Health Profile', in Walker and Rosser (eds.), *Quality of Life Assessment*, 111–30, at 97.
14 Marjorie Kagawa-Singer, 'Redefining health: living with cancer', *Social Science and Medicine*, 37 (3) (1993), 295–304, at 295.
15 John Harris, *The Value of Life* (London, Routledge, 1985), 100.

4
The law's impact

MERVYN LYNN

The law impacts upon those facing death analogously to its impact on the living well; it limits what they can do and what may lawfully be done to them. Law, whether as a result of parliamentary enactment or, more commonly in this sphere, by development of judge-made Common Law, can protect by imposing restraints upon the actions of others or by imposing a duty upon others to act to the benefit of the recipient.

In creating and developing standards of behaviour, the Common Law seeks to follow, or occasionally to lead, public opinion, as perceived by the judiciary. In the sphere of the treatment of the ill and the dying, the boundaries which the law imposes on the behaviour of others can frequently be seen to reflect views which can be traced to Judaeo-Christian teaching. These views are also discernible at the core of good medical practice. Good medical practice is, in turn, also a yardstick utilized by the judiciary in determining the scope of the duties of health-care professionals and the limits of medical interference.

Thus, there is a circular process in which the judges, in declaring conduct lawful – which in turn forms a baseline for good medical practice – look to see what medical practice and medical and ethical reasoning currently sanction.[1] What medical practice permits at any given time is a product both of ethical reasoning, drawn from traditional, and often religious, views, and of an interpretation of the law. The law can thus simultaneously lead and be led by medical practices. A concrete example of this is the well-known case of Anthony Bland, whose doctors had decided to cease treating and feeding him after several years in which he was in a persistent vegetative state. That responsible medical practitioners reached such a conclusion was instrumental in the High Court, the Court of Appeal and the House of Lords, all coming to the same conclusion; that it was not only good medical practice to withdraw feeding from patients who are irrevocably in PVS, but that it was also legally permissible. Indeed, some of their Lordships went so far as to declare that to continue to treat and feed someone who could derive no benefit from such actions would be unlawful, both as a civil trespass and as a criminal assault.[2] We will return to this landmark decision later in the chapter.

1 The dying competent adult

A competent adult who believes that his or her death is pending in the immediately foreseeable future may wish either to delay death for as long as possible or to accelerate it. Such a person may wish to take steps to achieve either of these ends which may involve the assistance of others.

The law generally permits any competent individual to expend his or her resources with few restrictions, except where it impacts adversely on others. However, whilst those who wish to expedite their own deaths may kill themselves, they may not lawfully engage the help of others to assist in what the law regards as self-killing. Since the enactment of the Suicide Act 1961, although it has ceased to be a criminal offence either to kill or to attempt to kill oneself, it remains an offence to assist someone else, or to procure another, to take his or her own life.[3]

As with nearly all criminal offences, an innocent actor who, without knowledge of the principal actor's motivation, unwittingly assists the principal in a way which helps the latter to bring about his own death, will not normally fall foul of the criminal law. Whether someone is an innocent agent in such a venture would ultimately be determined by a jury, based on the available evidence, applying a jury's common sense to the facts as established.

The effect of the offence of aiding and abetting another's suicide is to deprive a competent adult of the assistance which may be necessary to secure his or her peaceful death. This may prevent them from dying either at the time or in the manner which, as autonomous beings, they would have selected. Whilst it may be understandable that the law should not compel one individual to assist another to kill that other, it is not easy to defend the prohibition on a willing volunteer who understands another's wish to control and determine the time and style of his or her death and who is happy to facilitate that choice.

The law recognizes that sanctity of life, as a principle, cannot trump an individual's right to self-determination by their own unaided hand, so it is difficult to accept that as a principle it should deny willing help to an individual whose death will either only be possible with that help or will be made easier and better by it. It seems that behind the law's prohibition on assisting another who wishes his or her own death is a fear of encouraging to die those who do not wish to; or of overzealous help. There is undeniable scope for abuse of the old by the young; of the very ill by their greedy or tired carers; or of the easily persuaded by the manipulative. However, to deny what may appear to many to be their ultimate right of autonomy – to choose how and when they die – merely in order to ensure that there is not abuse of that entitlement, seems inadequate. Parents and guardians have rights of control over their children: for example, they can and do determine if and when their children receive medical treatment.[4] Clearly a parent could abuse this right, or duty, to the detriment of the child. This potential for abuse is recognized, and there are mechanisms for either by-passing the parent's right of veto by care or wardship proceedings, or to prosecute and punish those who abuse it.

Doctors are as subject to criminal liability as any other citizen. A doctor cannot therefore accede to a patient's request to accelerate the patient's death by doing anything which would achieve that objective, unless it is otherwise medically appropriate treatment. Since 1957, at least, the courts have accepted the lawfulness of actions or omissions which may, as a by-product of their primary goal, have the effect of accelerating a patient's death.[5] Drugs, such as morphine, used palliatively to curtail a dying patient's suffering, are, under certain conditions, known to expedite death.

It is in such double-effect situations that analysis of criminal liability becomes muddied. To intend either, to accelerate the death of a patient or to assist the patient to do so, would, *prima facie*, satisfy the state of mind required to prosecute for murder or aiding and abetting suicide. The meaning of intention is undefined in criminal law, but there is a wealth of case law to support two propositions which are germane to the establishment of intention.[6] Firstly, a person may intend to achieve more than one result; so that to intend to relieve pain does not preclude the establishment of an intention thereby, or as an unavoidable consequence, to accelerate death. Secondly, a person may intend that which she or he did not 'desire'. Since the idea of intending to achieve a result, which one does not wish to achieve, seems dysfunctional, to say the least, if not downright absurd, this must be read with the suffix 'for its own sake', if it is to make any sense. So read, it may appear to be virtually a restatement of the first proposition.

The same case law establishes that, where an actor foresees a particular result as a 'natural' consequence of the proposed action, or that it is foreseen as a 'virtually certain' result, then that is sufficient to enable a jury to conclude that the result was intended. It follows that it can be no defence to a charge of murder to argue that there was an ulterior purpose for the action, if death was foreseen as the virtually certain outcome of the action. However, this realization lies uneasily with the previously identified judicial acceptance of the principle of double effect in relation to the administration of palliative drugs which are known to accelerate death as a virtual certainty. It may be that only where there is no possible therapeutic purpose achievable by the action – as in the case of Dr Cox – that a jury would conclude that the action of a health-care professional which resulted in death (and which that professional recognized would do so as a virtual certainty) was intended to kill and thus was murder.

In practice, health-care professionals who act in ways which will cause the death of their patients to be accelerated, are not prosecuted if there is evidence to show that their behaviour was compatible with good medical practice as having either an otherwise therapeutic purpose, or was in the best interests of their patients. If however, as in the 1992 case of Dr Cox,[7] the actions can have no such purpose and are, on the evidence, designed to hasten death, then, notwithstanding either the patient's wish for death to be hastened or that the doctor is motivated by the greatest degree of compassion, the doctor will be guilty of causing the patient's death. If discovered, such a doctor would be liable to face a prosecution for manslaughter or murder.

In situations not involving the death of a patient, it is possible for a doctor (like any other individual) to argue that the circumstances in which he or she acted were such as to make those actions necessary, even though *prima facie* criminal. In 1993 Dr Biezanek successfully thwarted a prosecution for supplying cannabis to her daughter who suffered from an unspecified condition for which, Dr Biezanek claimed, only cannabis brought relief.[8] Her counsel argued that she acted out of necessity in order to save her daughter's life. In 1985 Victoria Gillick sought to secure a declaration that it would be unlawful for a GP to supply a minor female, under the age of sexual consent, with contraception or contraceptive advice without the consent of her parent or guardian. In a case which went all the way to the House of Lords,[9] one of the arguments presented was that for a doctor to so act would be to aid and abet the offence of unlawful sexual intercourse, since that would be one of the natural consequences of the minor female using contraception. Not only would it be a natural consequence, but one which any doctor would recognize as a natural consequence. Therefore, the doctor would possess a state of mind sufficient to prosecute her or him as an accomplice to the offence of unlawful sexual intercourse which would be committed by the man with whom the female minor patient had sexual intercourse.

In rejecting this argument, the House of Lords demonstrated, not for the first time, the judicial willingness to let health-care professionals off the hook on grounds of pragmatism. The doctor's purpose, said their Lordships, would be to prevent an unwanted pregnancy, rather than to encourage or aid the act of unlawful sexual intercourse which would be a prerequisite to such a pregnancy. It is difficult to envisage a court accepting this ulterior-motivation argument from a non-medical defendant, in circumstances where there is no denial of the criminal outcome or of the help which the defendant's act represented to the perpetrator of the criminal act.

The case was also significant for the light which it shed on judicial views of the members of the medical profession. Noteworthy is Lord Scarman's view[10] that the *bona fide* exercise by a doctor of his medical judgment was the very negation of the state of mind required by the criminal law for conviction of an accomplice. In other words, if it was *bona fide* by medical standards it *could* not contravene the criminal law. In its context, the remark came close to implying that in practising medicine doctors were above criminal liability. If, however, we analyse the statement, it is clearly tautological, for if a doctor's conduct would be contrary to the criminal law, it necessarily cannot be *bona fide* behaviour. The criminal law provides no general immunity to doctors to engage in criminal conduct for good reasons or for bad; as the conviction of Dr Cox reaffirmed. This is, of course, subject to the defence of necessity, as discussed, above which may permit actions which, outside the circumstances inducing the necessity to act, would be unlawful. Necessity, however, cannot be used as a defence to a charge of murder,[11] except where the killing was necessitated by the need to save one's own life.

2 Acts versus omissions

The criminal law only infrequently imposes an obligation to act, as opposed to an obligation to desist from action. One of the instances where it does so is where there is identified a duty to act. This may be a result of a contract or of a special relationship existing between two or more people. Regardless of any specific contractual term between doctors and either their employers or their patients, it is clear that all doctors have such a relationship with those whom they accept as their patients. This duty may mandate certain actions in certain circumstances.

Where the patient is competent, the doctor's minimum duty is to avoid either action or an omission which would constitute 'gross negligence'. A doctor who fails to avoid such and who is thereby responsible for the death of a patient can face a charge of manslaughter[12] or, if the action or omission was intended to cause the patient's death, a charge of murder. (Providing the patient does not die, there is probably no criminal offence committed by the merely grossly negligent doctor, regardless of the harm which results.)[13]

What constitutes 'gross negligence' is undefined in criminal law and is left for the trial jury, guided by the judge's summing up, to decide. It is clear that within a medical context – and nearly all of the reported cases involve health-care personnel – a very great departure from proper practice and standards is required before a jury will be encouraged to convict a doctor of manslaughter on the grounds of gross negligence.[14] Three recent convictions were reviewed in two separate appeals.[15] These appellate courts have provided guidance for future juries which, though far from clear, indicates that the behaviour needed to constitute gross negligence must be extreme behaviour and far greater than would be needed to satisfy the civil law's requirements for negligence.

3   Civil law

Thus far, the effect only of the criminal law has been examined as a mechanism of control and restraint upon the acts or omissions of doctors, but the civil law also, by determining what is acceptable and unacceptable medical practice, operates as a constraint upon the behaviour of health-care professionals.

The law of trespass prevents any treatment or invasion which involves a touching of the patient's body without consent, providing that the patient is competent either to consent or to refuse the treatment or invasion. Trespass, which has its criminal counterpart in assault and battery, enshrines the principle that competent individuals have total and complete control over permission for any and all bodily interference with their person. It prohibits, upon the same pain of an action for financial damages, forcibly injecting a patient, as it does the bestowing of an unwanted kiss. The consent of a competent recipient is however a complete defence, except where the law denies the recipient the right to consent.

Long-standing statutory prohibitions on certain transactions with factually consenting minors have recently been supplemented by a ruling of the House of Lords[16] that even a competent adult cannot consent to being the recipient of actual bodily harm outside certain specified and recognized exceptions, all of which were said to be 'in the public interest'. Amongst these was 'reasonable surgical interference'.[17]

Although the concept of what is reasonable is capable of changing over time and within varying circumstances, it is clear that, for example, surgery which involves transplanting vital organs from a living person is not presently viewed as reasonable.

It would therefore matter neither that the donor wished the transplantation to take place, and freely consented, nor that the saving of the life of the recipient might be viewed as in the public interest. It would, at present, be unlawful if it resulted in the death of the donor. It would be killing the donor and, as such, an assault, a trespass and, of course, murder. Yet the idea of transplanting the organs of, say, an irrevocably comatose patient or an anencephalic neonate might make sound ethical (and financial) sense in a situation of scarce resources. It is foreseeable that a court will, possibly quite soon, be asked to declare transplantation from such an individual to be lawful. If a court were so to declare, it would then be logically possible to argue that what can be done without consent, in the case of an incompetent, irrevocably comatose, patient, ought to be something to which a competent patient, should be able to give valid consent. However, as the decision in Bland's case demonstrated, logic is not always a necessary feature or prerequisite of judicial decision-making.[18]

Within a medical context, there are no reported decisions of what constitutes reasonable surgical interference, but, for example, surgery which was performed solely in order to render someone unfit to serve in the armed forces would be contrary to public interest and therefore outside the exception.[19] *A fortiori* surgery designed to cause the recipient's death would also not be reasonable.

We have strayed back into criminal liability here and it is time to return and further examine the civil law as a restraint upon how doctors may treat the dying. There is a civil tort of negligence which has, at its core, the concept of reasonableness. Negligence requires proof of loss or injury arising from, and caused by, a breach of a duty of care owed to the injured person. Between a health-care professional and a patient there is undoubtedly such a duty of care; a duty not to cause foreseeable harm.[20] In determining whether that duty has been breached, the courts ask the injured party (the plaintiff) to prove, on the balance of probabilities, that no reasonable person in the same calling as the alleged tort feasor (the defendant) would have acted, or failed to act, as he or she acted, or failed to act. The yardstick, known as the '*Bolam* Rule', effectively allows the medical profession to dictate its own standards of care and treatment.

For, so long as others in the profession would have behaved to the plaintiff as the defendant did, then the courts will in general not hold that behaviour negligent. Only in rare and exceptional circumstances will the courts adjudicate between two or more schools of thought as to which is better medical practice.[21]

Precisely because it can be so difficult to establish negligence, in the absence of the clearest evidence of it – where the evidence speaks for itself (*res ipsa loquitur*) – the tort of negligence would not seem to be a strong restraint on health-care professionals' behaviour. In fact, there is a surprising degree of fear of negligence actions among members of the medical profession. This fear is disproportionate to the likelihood of such actions being successfully pursued against them. All NHS employees are indemnified against such claims, so the actions are in effect defended by health authorities or the insurance organizations who specialize in such indemnification.

Although it was a criminal trial and the charge was attempted murder, the case of *Leonard Arthur* in 1981 provides an extreme example of how, seemingly, even the most aberrant behaviour by a doctor can find others to support it, and thus to preclude the establishment of negligence in civil actions. Dr Arthur, at the request of the parents, withheld nutrition from a new-born suffering from Down's Syndrome, with the expectation and intention that it would die within a brief period – as indeed it did. Eminent paediatricians took the witness stand to give evidence of the acceptability of Dr Arthur's actions, which had included the administration of an analgesic and sedative to the neonate in order to prevent it indicating its hunger.

The case is additionally illustrative of the strong significance which the judges accord to the acceptability of behaviour within the medical profession in determining whether that behaviour crosses the boundary of legality. In the *Arthur* case the jury heard the trial judge tell them:

> you will think long and hard before deciding that doctors of the eminence we have heard, representing to you what medical ethics are, and apparently have been over a period of time in that great profession, have evolved standards which are tantamount to committing a crime.[22]

The jury obligingly found the defendant not guilty of attempting to murder the neonate, whose regime of non-treatment, designed to end its life, Dr Arthur had ordered and implemented. In the House of Commons the Attorney General said that the decision did not represent any change in the law of murder.

4 The incompetent patient

A patient whose death is imminent or foreseeable may, by virtue of that condition, or another, be unable either to give consent to treatment or to express a wish about the withholding of treatment. Such a patient is legally incompetent. Incompetence may be a product of a medical condition or of immaturity, whether intellectual or biological, or both.

Until the age of eighteen children are considered minors in law, although by statute from the age of 16 they can give full consent to any medical treatment.[23] Below that age they *may* be able to give consent, depending upon whether they are capable of understanding the nature of the proposed treatment or medical invasion, its risks and benefits to them, and of alternatives. Whether a child is so capable will depend both upon the complexity of what needs to be understood and the intellectual capability of the child, which may of course be affected by the existence of the medical condition which calls for the treatment. A child who is dying risks being viewed as unable to comprehend the emotional concept of death, which adults so frequently cannot easily come to terms with, and therefore not competent to make a decision which would hasten or delay that death. A parent or guardian would then be invited to decide, but, of course, this precludes the autonomy of the child and their decision need not necessarily reflect the wishes, if any, of the child. A parent may wish to try every possible treatment option in order to prolong a child's life, but it is the child who endures the invasion and pain of those options. A child, like an adult, is entitled to say, 'I've had enough, I don't wish to fight any longer.' A child expressing such a wish is entitled to have that wish respected by doctors, regardless of contrary parental views.

It is not only in the case of a child deemed incompetent that parental preferences may prevail. In 1991 the Court of Appeal held[24] that the refusal of treatment, by even a competent minor, could be overridden by health-care professionals if a parent or guardian gives consent to that which the competent child refuses. Under the age of eighteen, therefore, no minor can be viewed as truly autonomous, for though their consent to treatment will render that treatment lawful, their refusal, by comparison, carries very little legal weight, since it can be vetoed by a parent or guardian. That said, a health-care professional must take account of the refusal of a competent minor in deciding whether to go ahead with the proposed treatment. To treat in circumstances where it would be unreasonable to do so would constitute negligence, though not trespass. Health-care professionals, however, may be easily persuaded by articulate parents that their views should prevail over those of a dying child. The right, of anyone with parental responsibility for a child, to give consent for medical treatment of that child is a product of the duty owed by that person to the child. Accordingly, the duty must be exercised in the best interests of the child, and any consent which can be shown to be contrary to the child's best interests would be an *ultra vires* exercise of parental responsibility and therefore void. A doctor acting on the basis of such consent would act unlawfully: there being no true consent to the treatment, it would constitute a trespass.

At first, it may appear unlikely that a doctor would not only propose treatment which would not be in the child's best interests, but that a parent would also consent to it. However, this depends on how we interpret the best interests of another. We know, or believe we know, what is, and what is not, in our own best interests and may too easily infer that this applies *mutatis mutandis* to a child. To many adults the idea of suicide is unthinkable or incomprehensible, the desire to die alien to them. It might be very difficult for such adults to recognize the possibility that their child could hold a contrary view. They, of course, are not living the life from which the child might seek escape, nor may they share the fearlessness with which a child may face death.

The decision in the *Bland* case has firmly established that the treatment of incompetent adult patients is also subject to the same test of 'best interests'.[25] As with children, there is a danger that it is spuriously clear what their best interests are. Yet precisely because they are incompetent, it may be extremely difficult to see what might be in the best interests of those individuals. 'If I had terminal cancer/Down's Syndrome, I know what I would/would not want' ignores the crucial reality that the speaker does not, in fact, suffer from the condition and may only inadequately be able to imagine what it would be like to suffer from it.

Where the incompetent patient has previously been competent and has expressed a view as to how they wish to be treated as the end approaches, then, depending on whether the actual prevailing circumstances match those previously envisaged by the patient, it may be appropriate to be guided by those previously expressed views in deciding whether or how to treat the patient in the terminal phase of life.[26]

The person who attempts suicide but who is discovered in a rescuable condition presents an obvious example of the difficulty of determining another person's best interests. To some, the suicide attempt will be a 'cry for help' and not a serious intentional act of attempted self-destruction. To others, it will be a product of disordered thinking, indicating that it was not a competently or autonomously made decision, whilst to yet others the act may be *prima facie* evidence of a desire to die which the individual had autonomously decided was in his or her best interests. If the latter view prevails, then logically any treatment to rescue the patient will not be in that patient's best interests and, that being so, such endeavours would be unlawful. This would be so, notwithstanding that they may have been necessary to save the patient's life. In such a case the patient ought to be permitted to die from the self-inflicted harm. If either of the former views prevails, then it *would* be in the patient's best interests to be treated and restored to health.

In practice, it will be rare that there is clear and hard evidence of a definite, settled intention to die, and remedial treatment is likely to be embarked upon. One of the consequences of the law's prohibition on helping someone to commit suicide is that many are forced to attempt it alone. The evidence of their intention to kill themselves, which an accomplice could provide, is thus rarely available, for even 'suicide notes' can be faked, or coerced from the victim, by a potential murderer.

Successful suicides involve feelings of anger, frustration and guilt in those who witness them or who are left to live with the consequences of them. Not surprisingly, perhaps, we are often

loath to accept the validity of suicide as an expression of autonomy. The temptation to believe that there must have been a
preferable alternative to self-destruction is common and, in
consequence, there is likely to be a strong inclination to accept
that it would be in the best interests of a suicide attempter to be
given another chance. Yet the horror of awakening to more of the
'hell on earth' which one thought one had left behind, rather than
to the 'heaven' to which one thought one was going, is scarcely
imaginable, and difficult to view as being in anyone's best interests. The only way in which it is possible to maximize the chance
of one's death wishes being respected when one is no longer
capable of expressing them, is to make an advanced directive (a
'living will'), which we examine later in this chapter.

Anthony Bland, after several years in PVS, was a paradigm
example of the incompetent patient. As far as was ascertainable,
he was totally insensate. As such, it was all but impossible to
claim that he had any interests, best or otherwise. This did not
stop some of the appellate judges who heard the case (brought by
the hospital trust who owned the hospital in which he was cared
for) trying to do so. The more robust among them, however,
correctly identified that he could have no best interests because
he had no interests at all.[27] Whether he lived or died was irrelevant to him, because he would be unaware of either situation. No
attempt was made to evaluate the benefits of any post-death existence which Anthony Bland might have.

Precisely because he had no best interests to be served by any
medical treatment, all medical treatment designed to continue
his existence – and the courts held that this included feeding him
– was treatment which, because it was *not* in his best interests and
because he could not consent to it, would be unlawful. It would
represent a tortious trespass in civil law and least an assault, if
not grievous bodily harm, in criminal law.

The logic of the courts' reasoning in *Bland* should lead inexorably to the deaths of all long-term patients in PVS whose
condition was diagnosed as irrevocable. For to continue to treat,
or invasively feed, such patients is to act in a manner which,
because it is not in the best interests of those patients, and is not
consented to, is unlawful. At the time of the case it was estimated
that there were over 1,000 such patients in hospitals throughout
Britain.[28]

In reality, many of these patients will probably continue to be fed and treated. Whether they will follow Bland into eternity or remain insensate in their hospital beds will, we suspect, depend on the views and wishes of their relatives (Bland's parents wished for his death) and the financial constraints within the health authority or trust. Keeping patients alive unnecessarily, possibly even unlawfully alive, is an obvious expense which could be avoided by those seeking to make better use of limited resources.[29]

Nor is the decision in *Bland* logically or inexorably confined to patients in irrevocable PVS. It is possible to argue that certain medical conditions, though not immediately fatal in themselves, cause such extreme suffering and give rise to such a demonstrably awful and low quality of life that it is not in the sufferer's best interests to continue to suffer.[30] Thus treatment designed to stabilize or maintain the sufferer's condition is not lawful because it is treatment which fails the best-interests test. This presupposes (which may not always be the case) that the sufferer cannot consent to the treatment, or refuse it, and has not previously indicated, by means of an advanced directive, that he or she wished to continue to be treated.

It is important to stress that, for any patient, the question of what treatment they will be offered, or whether they will be offered any treatment, is almost exclusively a matter of clinical-judgement by the health-care professional in charge of the case. There is no absolute entitlement to treatment, and unless it can be demonstrated that no reasonable health-care professional would refuse treatment (in which case to not treat would be negligent), a patient cannot demand treatment.[31] Obviously, any private contractual arrangement between doctor and patient could include such an express entitlement to specified treatment. Otherwise doctors are free to determine, on criteria known only to themselves, whether to treat, or how to treat, any individual patient. Increasingly, a scarcity of resources will play a part in such decision-making. Is there a bed? Is there a cheaper alternative? Is it worth it, in terms of the length and level of benefits which successful treatment would produce in the patient? A cost-benefit analysis might suggest that keeping the dying alive a little longer may not be a sound use of limited resources. It must be emphasized that in such decision-making the views of the patients or their relatives have no necessary role. That said, a patient may, by refusing to consent to one type of treatment, encourage a doctor to suggest another which is preferable to the patient; but there is no obligation upon a doctor to offer the patient who refuses treatment any alternative – except where it would be negligent to fail to do so.[32.] There is a growing body of case law in which the country's most senior judges acknowledge the legitimacy of doctors taking account of a scarcity of resources in the exercise of their clinical judgement whether to treat particular patients.[33]

5 Advance directives

The idea of determining in advance how one would prefer to be treated, and especially how one would *not* wish to be treated in future, but foreseen, circumstances has gained prominence with the spread of Aids. Those diagnosed as either HIV positive or suffering from Aids can readily envisage their dying. There is already evidence that the terminal stages may be extremely painful. Taking the opportunity to indicate what treatment one would be prepared to receive, or not receive, and up to what stages of deterioration, was promoted by the Terrence Higgins Trust. In association with King's College, London, the Trust, among others, has produced a 'living will' form which can be completed by an Aids sufferer, or anyone else, in conjunction with his or her medical advisers, in which he or she expresses future treatment hopes and limitations.

In 1993 the legality of such an advanced directive was established in the case of *Re C*,[34] in which the High Court resolutely upheld the binding nature of a competently expressed wish upon those who, in the future, were made aware of it. However, those who wish to execute such a document, with the expectation that it will bind future carers, will need to be able to identify with some degree of specificity both the circumstances in which the directive will become operative and the nature of what they are willing or unwilling to undergo. We remain sceptical as to the future likelihood of the judiciary, perhaps, too easily finding a *lacuna* in such a document, which is all too likely to have been completed without expert legal advice. This would permit a judge to declare the document not to be binding, because the circumstances in which it was envisaged to operate are not sufficiently close to those prevailing at the time when its operation is being considered, or that the treatment options now available at the time when the living will is envisaged as coming into operation were unknown and unknowable at the time of the document's construction. The wise testator will update and revise a living will, with his or her doctor's advice and help.

There must also be fears concerning genuine changes of mind. Will an oral revocation of the written document, at the time when the document would otherwise have become operable, suffice to override it? Will a patient who earlier signed for no treatment be able to consent to it validly years later when the true imminence of death causes a changed perspective? The BMA, not surprisingly, wants such advance directives to be put on a statutory footing.

6 Transplantation

As the certainty of death's approach increases, the idea of penance, or making amends for past misdeeds, is probably not uncommon. Altruism may take many forms, one of which may be organ donation.

Whilst there is no legal impediment to anyone giving permission for the use of their organs after their death, the medical reality is that the process of dying may render certain vital organs unusable. This is particularly the case with, for example, anencephalic neonates. Intensive drug therapy, designed to delay death, may likewise impact negatively on the re-usability of vital organs. To permit such organs to be removed before death is presently unlawful. Indeed, insofar as the removal would cause death, it would be murder.

Yet to die whilst undergoing a nephrectomy or other surgical procedure designed to remove and re-use vital organs, might be an acceptable form of self-determination for many. Such surgical death combines the sought-for release from the lingering terminal phase of life with a priceless gift of altruism by which others may live. From a medical point of view such surgery, although directly leading to the death of the donor, has none of the purely destructive qualities of a lethal injection of a noxious, non-therapeutic substance. Nor is it devoid of therapeutic value – albeit not to the donor. It would be surgery carried out for a socially useful purpose, which could be compared favourably to regimes of non-treatment whose objective is to cause death but to do so without any deliberate act which induces death.[35] Such non-treatment regimes may, or may not, cause pain to the dying, but clearly do cause pain to those forced to watch the slow process of those whom they loved, or cared for, starving to death.

7 Conclusion

It is clear that the principal effect of judicial interpretations of both civil and criminal law is to maximize the freedom of action and discretion of the medical profession, in its treatment decision-making, with respect to the ill and the dying. Whilst a doctor must not act negligently, this represents a minimal restraint so long as members of the profession effectively determine the legally acceptable standards of reasonable treatment and reasonable non-treatment.

To this general conclusion there is one significant exception. It is that doctors may never act in a positive, purposeful manner in order exclusively to accelerate a patient's death. The law, however, will sanction coincidental, but inevitable, hastening of death as a consequence of any reasonable therapeutic intervention. It also sanctions regimes of non-treatment, or deliberate omissions, the result of which, and the purpose of which, is to accelerate death; providing only that such is reasonable as being within existing, accepted medical practice.

From the perspective of the dying patient, the law seems to adopt a very partisan position. The doctors can effectively determine how and when the patient dies, either by treating or not treating the patient in a given way. The patients, by contrast, are denied this final autonomous exercise of self interest. True, they can, by refusing food or treatment necessary for survival, hasten their death, but they are denied the right to determine precisely how and when they will die if the execution of such decision-making involves assistance. Realistically, the scope for self-destruction, especially within the controlled and monitored environment of a health-care institution, and which does not involve the assistance or acquiescence of those employed therein, may be slim. All the more so if we recognize that the dying are very likely to be in a physically debilitated state.[36] The law denies those who wish to have control over the manner and time of their death the help and sympathy which may clearly be vital. That it is denied to them, within the very institutions in which that caring assistance might reasonably be expected to be available, seems curiously cruel. That there might be scope for abuse of such a power demands that mechanisms of control be established to minimize that abuse. It is surely not beyond the competence of our legislators to devise and implement such controls – and sooner rather than later.[37]

Notes

1 See *R* v. *Arthur* (1981) 12 BMLR 1 and *Airedale NHS Trust* v. *Bland* [1993] 1 All ER 859.
2 See Lord Mustill, op. cit., 894.
3 S.3.
4 S.3 The Children Act 1989. See also the *Gillick* case, below n.9.
5 *R* v. *(Bodkin) Adams* [1957] Crim L.R. 365.
6 See *R* v. *Moloney* [1985] 1 All ER 1025 HL and *R* v. *Nedrick* [1986] 3 All ER 1 CA.
7 *R* v. *Cox* (1992) 12 BMLR 38.
8 *The Times,* 14 October 1993.
9 *Gillick* v. *West Norfolk AHA* [1985] 3 All ER 402.
10 At p. 425.
11 *R* v. *Dudley and Stevens* (1884) 14 QBD 273.
12 *R* v. *Adomako* [1994] 2 All ER 79 HL.
13 Though dicta in the nineteenth-century case of *R* v. *Curtis* (1885) 15 Cox CC 746 at 752 suggested that one who causes bodily injury by neglect would be criminally liable.
14 See *R* v. *Bateman* (1925) 19 Cr. App. R.8.
15 In *R* v. *Prentice and Shulman* [1993] 4 All ER 935, the Court of Appeal quashed the manslaughter convictions of two doctors who had recklessly caused an intravenous injection to be administered intrathecally despite clear instructions indicating its correct course of administration. In *R* v. *Adomako* (above) the House of Lords upheld the manslaughter conviction of an anaesthetist who had failed to monitor his patient's oxygen supply.
16 *R* v. *Brown and Others* [1993] 2 All ER 75 HL.
17 At p.98 Lord Lowry cites, with approval, this phrase used by Lord Lane CJ in a 1981 case. Lord Jauncey referred to 'necessary surgery'

at p.88. Lord Mustill referred to 'proper medical treatment' being 'in a category of its own' (at p.110).

18 Lord Browne-Wilkinson recognized the inherent absence of a logical distinction between allowing someone, whose death had been determined to be in his or her best interests, to die slowly by omission, and bringing about that good death by a positive act. See op. cit., 884.

19 The historical Common Law offence of maiming is well documented. See Smith and Hogan, *Criminal Law*, 7th edn (1992), 409. In *Brown* Lord Mustill questioned whether it is currently an offence, op. cit., 106.

20 See dicta of Lord Hewart CJ in *Bateman*, op. cit., 12.

21 In *Sidaway* v. *Governors of Bethlem Royal Hospital and Maudsley Hospital* [1985] 1 All ER 643, the House of Lords recognized that in rare and extreme situations the courts *would* evalute differing schools of medical thought. The recent case of *Smith* v. *Tunbridge Wells HA* [1994] 5 Med LR 334 and the under-reported earlier case of *Hucks* v. *Cole* (1968) 112 Sol. Jol. 483 are solitary examples of judicial willingness to do so.

22 Op. cit., 22.

23 Family Law Reform Act 1969.

24 *Re R.* [1991] 4 All ER 117 CA.

25 The House of Lords had first identified this test in *F* v. *West Berkshire HA* [1989] 2 All ER 545 HL.

26 See below on Advanced Directives.

27 See Lord Mustill, op. cit., 894.

28 There have been at least two further court declarations that it would be lawful to withdraw essential life-supporting treatment. *Frenchay Healthcare NHS Trust* v. *S* [1994] 2 All ER 403 and *Swindon and Marlborough NHS Trust* v. *S*, *Guardian* Law Report, 10 December 1994.

29 It has been estimated that it may possibly cost in excess of £100 million per year to care for 1,000 PVS patients.

30 In the case of *Re J* [1990] 3 All ER 930, the Court of Appeal recognized that not treating so as to cause the death of a five-month-old girl with very severe physical and mental handicap would be in her best interests.

31 See *R* v. *Secretary of State for Social Services ex parte Hincks* (1980) 1 BMLR 93 CA. See also Lord Donaldson MR in *Re J*, op. cit., 934.

32 A patient might refuse a particular treatment for religious reasons in circumstances where the alternative treatment, which would be consented to, is much more expensive. See 'When others suffer for your faith' (*Independent*, 25 October 1994).

33 See for example Lord Donaldson MR in *Re J*, op. cit., 934, and Lord Mustill in the *Bland* case, op. cit., 893. Lord Brown-Wilkinson, in the same case, thought it was an issue which Parliament needed to consider – see p.879.

34 (1993) BMLR 77.

35 Such regimes featured in the *Arthur* case and in the *Bland* case.

36 A reported survey of 273 (out of 312) doctors who answered the question, indicated that 60 per cent of doctors have received requests from patients to hasten their death (*Guardian*, 20 May 1994).

37 The State of Oregon was the first in the world to enact legislation to enable competent adults who are dying, to be supplied with lethal dosages of non-therapeutic drugs to bring about death by their own hands – The Death With Dignity Act 1994. In February 1994, an all-party House of Lords Select Committee on Medical Ethics unanimously rejected calls for the introduction of legislation to legalize euthanasia in Britain.

5
Ethical decision-making in palliative care: the clinical reality

ILORA FINLAY

1 Introduction

The clinical practice of palliative care involves the care of patients who are facing death. The World Health Organization has defined palliative care as follows: 'Palliative care is the active total care of patients whose disease is not responsive to curative treatment.' Control of pain, of other symptoms, and of psychological, social and spiritual problems, is paramount. The goal of palliative care is achievement of the best quality of life for patients and their families. Many aspects of palliative care are also applicable earlier in the course of the illness in conjunction with anti-cancer treatment.

Many patients cannot be cured at the time of diagnosis and therefore require a palliative approach to their care from the outset. Cancers such as cancer of the lung or pancreas, and neurological diseases such as motor neurone disease carry a very poor prognosis and respond poorly or not at all to treatment aimed at modifying the disease process. For many other cancers, for example metastatic breast cancer, treatment aims to control the disease and thence the symptoms; it may slightly prolong life but will not cure. As the disease progresses, symptoms tend to worsen and be more frequent, so the patients need more specialist palliative care intervention to maintain quality of life, to live actively until death rather than feeling debilitated and waiting to die. The patient requirements of palliative care from the time of diagnosis to death can be represented by the following diagram.

CONTINUATION OF THE PALLIATIVE CARE PROCESS

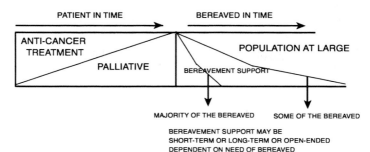

During this time there are many clinical decisions to be taken, and therefore applied ethics is part of routine daily practice. A clear example occurs in palliative care when philosophy and theory of ethical thinking are translated into clinical decision-making and directly affect the patient. Simply put, it is the ethical framework behind clinical decision-making that steers 'life-and-death' decisions.

It is therefore important that the clinician has a clear framework in his or her head to apply to each decision. In most contexts the term 'clinician' is considered to apply only to the doctor, but this is a fallacy. It is all the professionals in the multi-disciplinary team i.e. doctors, nurses, physiotherapists, occupational therapists, social workers and chaplains who must understand ethics in order to make responsible decisions as a team. It is the application of ethical theory to decision-making, particularly the principles of autonomy, beneficence, non-maleficence and justice, that will be dealt with in this chapter.

2 Trust

The relationship between the clinician and the patient can only function as a support relationship if it is founded on trust. The patient entrusts his or her care, and thereby his or her life, to the skill of the professionals, principally the doctors and nurses, who are responsible for providing care. This trust is crucial to understanding the duties of the professional towards the patient.

The General Medical Council's Education Committee

published recommendations in October 1987. These identified the attributes of the independent practitioner and outlined the duties of the doctor. These guidelines list the attributes that must be acquired in a doctor's professional development. This document highlights the precise attributes that patients are looking for in a doctor, without which the trust that the patient puts in the doctor would be betrayed. These include:

- the ability to solve clinical and other problems in medical practice
- possession of adequate knowledge and understanding of the body and mind in health and disease, and a higher standard of knowledge and skills in a doctor's speciality
- communication skills, which include sensitive and effective communication
- the ability to exercise sound clinical judgement
- the ability to recognize and analyse ethical problems.

These and other requirements are amplified in the document. However, it is clearly stated that 'good medical practice depends on the partnership between the doctor and the patient based on mutual understanding and trust; the doctor may give advice but the patient must decide whether to accept this.'

This trust also extends to other members of the team. A patient trusts that decisions or actions by the doctor and nurse are taken with the best of intention and with the patient's best interest at heart. It is precisely because of this inherent relationship of trust that any failure by professionals to act according to a moral and ethical code is so damaging to patients and rightly engenders anger. Any possibilities for doctors or nurses to abuse their professional position must therefore be guarded against rigorously.

There can be times when a patient can fail to express clearly a view, or relatives may try to pressurize professionals into action through intentional malice to the patient. The patient must know that he or she will always be respected as an individual, and that others will not be able to influence care adversely.

The Association for Palliative Medicine is a group of doctors whose professional role is to care for terminally ill patients, whether they are dying from cancer, Aids or other diseases. The curriculum for training lays out some ethical principles that underlie good palliative medicine. They are based on the four key principles of autonomy, beneficence, non-maleficence and justice, that will be discussed in this chapter. However, before going on to that discussion, it is worth stating the ethical principles that should be acquired by every medical student and should be inherent in every doctor's training whatever the speciality.

The doctor should demonstrate respect for the patient ('autonomy') by:
agreeing priorities and goals with the patient and carers,
discussing treatment options with the patient and jointly formulating care plans,
not withholding information desired by the patient at the request of a third party,
fulfilling the patient's needs for information about any treatments respecting the patient's wish to decline treatment.

The doctor should show respect for life and acceptance of death by understanding that:
treatment should never have the induction of death as its specific aim,
a doctor has neither right nor duty, legal or ethical, to prescribe a lingering death.

The doctor should:
understand the issues which surround requests for euthanasia,
recognize the dangers of professionals making judgements based on factors such as pre-morbid disability or age.

3   Autonomy

The term 'autonomy', meaning self-rule or self-government is derived from Greek. It is important to remember that autonomy exists only if it can be exercised, so that an individual has autonomy only when able to implement it. However, individuals in society cannot behave autonomously since they all interact with each other. There are times when the autonomous wishes of one individual may conflict with the autonomy of others in society, who interact with that individual. A clear example has been specified in the conscience clause of the 1968 Abortion Act where the autonomous wish of a woman to have an abortion could not force a gynaecologist, who conscientiously objects to the principle of abortion, to abort the fetus. Sadly, society has not adequately policed the conscience clause, so pro-life gynaecologists find it difficult to achieve promotion, since their peer group, who are undertaking abortions, will stand in the way of their promotion. In this case, the wish to share the workload of abortion requests appears to override respect of the individual's conscience. However, there are people who have achieved promotion whilst openly invoking the conscience clause.

If a patient is allowed to have autonomy, then those caring for the patient must show respect for the patient's autonomy and allow the patient to exercise autonomy in decision-making. Respect for the patient is shown by openly discussing treatment options, using language and terminology that are clearly understood by the patient. Such discussions must go at the patient's pace whenever possible. An agreed treatment plan, formulated between physician, patient and carers, is a powerful demonstration of respect. Respect for patients' autonomy is clearly demonstrated when a patient's request for information is answered, rather than that information being withheld at the request of a third party such as the patient's spouse or child; in other words a request to a doctor not to tell a patient the diagnosis may be a pointer to background family dynamics. It may help the physician when talking to the patient, but if this patient wishes to know the diagnosis then the physician, in respecting the patient's autonomous wishes for information, must discuss the diagnosis with the patient. So professionals must meet the patient's need for information when that information is requested. Meeting a patient's information needs entails using language clearly understood by the patient and does not give carers a licence to hand over information bluntly or insensitively, since that would be contrary to the principle of non-maleficence, so that any 'bad news' must be broken to the patient gently and sensitively, never denying the patient realistic hope. This concept of gentle sensitive imparting of information, whilst maintaining realistic hope, is along the principles of beneficence and non-maleficence.

Patients may wish to decline treatment offered. When this is an informed decision, professionals must respect the patient's decision and continue to care and support the patient in this action. For example, a patient may decline blood transfusion on religious grounds or may decline chemotherapy, feeling unwilling to undergo the side-effects such as hair loss, vomiting and sore mouth when the treatment will only slightly alter the course of the disease but will not be curative. There may be times when patients may wish to change their mind over treatment decisions previously made and they must be supported and respected in rediscussion of treatment options.

Dignity has been defined as having a sense of personal worth. The dignity of one person is not absolute, but depends on the way that people behave towards that person. A person treated with respect and dignity will have a sense of dignity, whereas a person treated disrespectfully or abused, who has been treated as worthless, will have less or no sense of personal dignity. The role of professional carers must be to enhance a person's sense of dignity at all times. Potentially distressing occurrences such as episodes of urinary or faecal incontinence must be minimized by carers so that they do not undermine the patient's sense of personhood. A simple example is the patient who has had an episode of urinary incontinence who could be asked, 'Did you wet yourself?' or 'Did the urine come away on its own?' The latter question implies that the principal fault is with the urine, and is less damaging to the patient's dignity than the former.

4 Informed consent

The principle of informed consent involves respect of patient autonomy: for patients to make informed decisions they must have adequate information. Part of the decision-making process involves the balance between the benefits of a proposed treatment and the risks and burdens of the treatment.

In everyday parlance, the weighing-up of the 'risks versus benefits' and 'burdens versus benefits' of a treatment have sometimes appeared to take second place to the pressure from the legal professions which pushes for 'everything to be done'. Those interested in litigation will always want to take the extreme model as the point of argument in order to win their case. Unfortunately this means that the concept of informed consent has been corrupted from being a balanced explanation to the patient of realistic risks against benefits. It has become replaced, particularly in the USA, by a defensive medical practice of informing the patient of every possible risk that might occur, however small, and thereby imposing a huge burden of anxiety on patients. Some would argue that this extreme view provides 'over information' and becomes unethical, since it burdens patients with unnecessary knowledge about side-effects which they are extremely unlikely to experience, and may prejudice their therapeutic response by greatly increasing anxiety levels. It also may impair a true respect of patient autonomy, since the patient is looking to the clinician for an expert opinion to provide balanced information rather than information weighted in favour of the physician's defence lawyers. In respecting autonomy, the physician has a duty to provide information relevant to that individual patient, and this duty includes attaching a weighting to the information in terms of most likely to extremely unlikely risks. However, any paternalism which belittles the patient's knowledge in comparison with the doctor's 'superior' knowledge must be avoided. A paternalistic attitude does not respect autonomy.

Consent is given by every patient every time they comply with medical instructions. It is not dependent on a signature on a piece of paper. A signed consent form is simply a witness to a verbal consent. The patient who agrees to swallow antibiotics is giving consent to the prescribed antibiotic treatment from the physician. A patient who refuses antibiotics is quite within his or her rights to do so, and should not be denied care or chastised for the wish to decline treatment if this is an informed decision; this patient is simply exercising his or her autonomous right to decline treatment.

Difficulties often arise over patients with advanced disease who develop a chest infection. In deciding whether or not an infection should be treated, the ethical principles outlined above should be implemented: i.e. does the patient want to have the infection treated, does the patient understand the consequences of non-treatment, are there risks attached to treating which are greater than the probable benefits? Is this patient likely to die of the underlying disease, and so is current imposition of antibiotic treatment futile, in that it will bring no sustainable benefit? Does the effort for the patient in taking the drug impose an undue burden which is greater than possible benefits? If the patient has distressing symptoms from a chest infection, then it is right to treat, since this will relieve distress, but it is not ethical to give the patient painful injections in so doing, since one pain will be imposed instead of another pain, and therefore the patient cannot be said to be benefiting overall. Intramuscular injections are a good example of a burdensome treatment, even though the drug being given carries low risk and is thought to do good. The burden of the intramuscular injection would make that treatment route unethical, but the oral route or the use of a painless established intravenous route could be justified. In the patient who does not have intravenous therapy, again the question must be asked whether the intravenous line is burdensome or is a futile treatment.

5 Beneficence and non-maleficence

Beneficence means 'doing good' and non-maleficence means 'doing no harm'. These are probably the most useful concepts in practical day-to-day clinical management, since they clarify thinking when decisions are difficult and patient autonomy has been fully respected. In simple terms, the benefits of a treatment should always outweigh the risks of treatment (to do good) and the burdens should be less than the predicted benefit (to do no harm).

It may be helpful to think about this balance by citing some clinical examples. Consider two patients, both of whom had cancer of the oesophagus (gullet), making them both unable to swallow nutrition. In both these patients lack of nutrition and fluid input was a major clinical problem. Both patients had a fine naso-gastric tube (tube going through the nose down into the stomach through which liquid feeds can be given). The first patient had several secondary deposits of cancer in the bones and liver and had severe nausea and vomiting. The naso-gastric tube had given him a sore throat. His wish was to rest in peace. Pain relief and drugs to control the vomiting could be given by an alternative route (via a syringe driver, which is a painless route). The patient was aware that removal of the naso-gastric tube would result in removal of a route for nutrition, but this was his wish, as the naso-gastric tube was a burden to him. The naso-gastric tube was removed, he was given adequate pain relief and anti-sickness medication, and died peacefully forty-eight hours later; his dying at that time was inevitable whatever the intervention. The naso-gastric tube was of no benefit to him since his other problems with his cancer were killing him, and it was a burdensome and futile treatment. Therefore there was no difficulty in ceasing the naso-gastric feeding. The inevitability of the man's death was not altered by the presence of the naso-gastric tube, but his quality of life was severely undermined by it, and his autonomous request was to cease treatment through it.

The second patient also had a sore throat from the naso-gastric tube and hated having to be fed through it. He also had some pain, which was controlled with morphine, again via a syringe driver. However his general condition was better, and he decided to agree to a simple operation (a gastrostomy) when a feeding tube was inserted directly through the abdominal wall into his stomach. This meant he no longer had a tube hanging out of his nose, which was unsightly, and all feeding and drugs could be given directly into the stomach. He quickly learnt to put his liquid food and drugs through this tube himself and soon was able to go out to the pub, feeling himself to be socially acceptable now he did not have a tube hanging out of his nose. Despite being very ill, he enjoyed a half-pint of beer by swilling some beer around his mouth and pouring the half-pint through a funnel into his stomach tube thereby obtaining the taste of the beer and letting the alcohol reach his brain. For him the benefits of the tube were much greater than the burdens of this inconvenient way of obtaining nutrition, and the risks of the operation were small compared to the anticipated benefits. Therefore in this man, with the same diagnosis and many of the same clinical problems, the ethical management was completely different.

6 Justice

The fourth important principle is that of justice. Justice has two domains: firstly there is justice to the individual, and secondly there is justice to society as a whole. Health-care professionals, and particularly physicians, have a dual responsibility in the justice of care given to the individual and the just allocation of resources.

The just care of an individual demands that no judgements are made on generalizations of any pre-existing condition. No patient should be judged as too old or having a previous disability which automatically excludes them from the right to treatment; the individual's personhood must be respected, and decisions over treatment must be made, weighing up the principles outlined above. Disabled persons, particularly those with difficulties with speech or hearing, which can impair communication, will need additional time and effort spent in ensuring that their autonomy is being respected; this is justice to the individual and it is their right.

Unfortunately resources in health care are finite and limited, so that justice demands that resources are allocated and used fairly for the overall benefit of those requiring them. A clear example of this is used in instances where there has been a major accident. Within the first hour or two of casualties arriving, decisions have to be made about which patients receive resuscitative measures such as blood transfusions and emergency surgery, and which can wait until more blood donors have been contacted or can wait for surgery a little later. There are also those casualties who will not be treated because their injuries are so severe and their chances of survival are so small that the time spent in attempts to resuscitate them will endanger the lives of others who have a better chance of survival. This is the principal of triage used on the battlefields and in the management of a major accident. However, patients with the same degree of injury may undergo active attempts at resuscitation and surgery in the attempt to save their life, should they be brought in as an isolated accident victim following a motor cycle or car accident. They probably will die in spite of medical intervention but, when they are the only person brought in it would be unethical to deny them the chance of life-saving treatment. The sad reality in the major accident is that there are not enough life-saving treatments to go round, and therefore decisions have to be made rapidly so that life-saving treatments are given to those with some chance of benefiting from them.

This is an extreme example, but in routine clinical practice doctors have decisions over resource allocation to make every day. Expensive new antibiotics cannot be used for every patient as the funds for drugs would rapidly be exhausted. So patients are given old-fashioned, cheaper antibiotics which have a high chance of success, even though there is a small chance that the bacteria may have developed resistance to them. Thus the expensive, rapidly effective, drugs are kept in reserve and the prescribing bill is reasonable, so that more patients can be treated within the same drug bill, and the development of drug resistance to the newer antibiotics is minimized.

7 The sanctity of life

Even within secular society, few would state that life in itself is worthless. Indeed, those expressing a global view that life has no intrinsic worth usually are suffering from a pathological depression and respond well to psychiatric treatment. The terrorist does not respect the sanctity of life.

Death is the natural and inevitable end to life, and medicine is unable to provide immortality. The physician has a constant dilemma between respecting the sanctity of life and striving to save life, whilst needing to respect death when it is inevitable. Respect for the sanctity of life demands that the physician never kills a patient. However, accepting death also demands that the physician adequately evaluates clinical decisions to ensure that futile, burdensome treatments are not imposed unnecessarily on a patient who is 'metabolically' dying. Therefore continuing to ventilate the patient who is brain-dead is a futile treatment; whilst not directly burdensome to the patient, who is already unaware of the situation, it is burdensome to the family in their grieving, and to society. It impairs the just allocation of resources, since the ventilator is then not available for other patients whose lives could be saved by its use. The decision to cease ventilation does not kill the patient, but does accept the inevitability of death.

This balance between respecting the sanctity of life and accepting death has been much argued over when principles of euthanasia are discussed. In many cases, the arguments are falsely distorted by those wishing to hold one standpoint or another. Issues surrounding requests for euthanasia will be dealt with in the following section.

Life is a fragile commodity, frequently undervalued by those able to enjoy a good quality of life who live in the belief that 'it will never happen to me' and undertake wildly risky activities, such as dangerous sports or irresponsible driving, in a mistaken denial of their own mortality. Death has a finality to it, often with unforeseen and unpredictable consequences for those remaining alive or 'left behind'. This awful finality and irreversibility of death is sometimes unrecognized in the philosophical debate of concepts. Whilst able to enjoy life and thinking, it is hard to imagine the world as it continues and in which, as individuals, we cease to exist. However, death is no respecter of age, creed or social class, and frequently cuts people off in their prime.

8   Advance directives

The introduction of legally binding advance directives in the United States has been driven, in part, by patients wanting to express their wishes, but to a large extent by doctors' fear of litigation. Without a signed advance directive the doctor is obliged to undertake cardiopulmonary resuscitation on patients even when death is anticipated. This situation fortunately does not arise in the UK, although there has been much debate about the instruction 'Not to be resuscitated' in patients' notes in hospitals. Where the patient's death is predictable and resuscitation would be futile, there is no obligation on the medical team to undertake cardiopulmonary resuscitation attempts. Indeed, it would be abhorrent to have the spectacle of people sitting round a dying patient and then, as the patient breathes for the last time, to have a crash team rushing in.

However, the role of the advance directive is useful in allowing open discussion between doctor and patient about their wishes and the consideration of various treatment options. In the majority of cases, the advance directive simply acts as a communication aid and promotes ethical debate over a patient's wishes, thereby enabling the principle of informed consent to be put into effect.

There are some problems with the intention signalled in an advance directive; these would become extremely obvious should the advance directive become legally binding. There are difficulties in drafting an advance directive whose wording is equally balanced between intervention and non-intervention. Currently there is no form that has found universal favour. There is difficulty in knowing whether the patient was competent, properly informed and free from duress at the time the directive was written; patients often do not disclose pressures which they may feel, and some degree of disordered thinking can be extremely difficult to detect clinically. Even when a patient has an advance directive written, it may be difficult to establish this fact, since patients do not keep them on their person at all times, and so, from a practical point, it is important that the intention contained in the advance directive is clearly recorded in a patient's case notes, rather than insisting on the advance directive itself being read. Even when the advance directive itself is available to be read through, there may be difficulty in interpreting the precise meaning of words. For example, there is no clear definition of terminal illness, and words such as 'recovery' can be interpreted differently as they may represent degrees of improvement which differ with interpretation from one person to another. This may lead to dispute over interpretation of wording, if the patient becomes incompetent and unable to express their wishes, and therefore there would need to be a mechanism for interpreting advance directives in dispute if they are to be legally binding. When it is viewed as a guide to care, the advance directive can be helpful as an additional piece of information to clinical decision-making, rather than allowing the wording to have overriding implications. It may be that the advance directive was written too long ago, or written with clinical expectations that have not occurred. An advance directive cannot prohibit normal care or measures for pain and symptom control; it would not be ethically right for a statement in an advance directive that specified that no life-prolonging treatments of any sort were to be given, and therefore to leave a patient to die a distressing death in cardiac failure when the administration of a diuretic could be both life-prolonging in terms of days and able to provide great symptom relief enabling the patient to die peacefully later.

There are also difficulties over defining competence as there are many levels of mental competency, and levels of cognitive functioning may vary from hour to hour or day to day in any patient who is severely ill. Within society there is an increasing tendency to say that dependency on others for care implies being a burden. However, there are many examples of people who have suffered extreme disability but then contributed greatly to society once they have adapted to their disability. This phase of adaptation can create many difficulties, since patients may feel despondent. They may despair and wish to die, and yet may later become very active with a life which they view as having quality and rewards. It is well recognized that a patient's perception of the quality of life varies from day to day, and the priorities within life also vary. In this situation, an advance directive, even if recently written may deny the patient access to full rehabilitative attempts. There is clear evidence from heart-attack and stroke patients that early active rehabilitation produces a much greater improvement than occurs with patients who do not receive intensive rehabilitation therapies such as physiotherapy. Treatment decisions, therefore, are not simply ones of whether to treat or not to treat, but must also include likely outcomes in the long term of deferred treatment should patients change their mind later. However, there are circumstances where a patient with a dense cardiovascular accident may have such neurological deficit that it is obvious that the chances of recovery are extremely poor. Under current practice such a patient would not be entered into an intensive rehabilitation programme as this would be futile. However, there is a danger that the advance directive could be seen as the only way in which treatment could be withheld from a patient, and therefore the effect (opposite to that intended by those who are proposing that advance directives become legally binding) could be that patients who have not signed an advance directive would have a greater rather than a reduced tendency to be overtreated.

In summary, the ability for patients to express in writing their wishes for care is a helpful aid to communication between doctor and patient. It can help patients start a dialogue of explanation to ensure that they have ample opportunity to express their wishes and that consent is informed when treatment decisions are taken. However, the concept of such an advance directive becoming legally binding has many problems and may not achieve the desired effect of a balanced ethical view in clinical decision-making.

9 Euthanasia

The term 'euthanasia' is used in everyday parlance to imply voluntary euthanasia i.e. the direct intentional killing of a person at his or her request as part of the medical care being offered. The word comes from Greek and implies 'a good death'. Therefore it is a travesty of the truth and sanitization of history to speak of 'involuntary euthanasia' as the mass murder and suffering inflicted in concentration camps. That was not euthanasia but mass murder.

It can be argued that the term 'euthanasia' cannot be used in relation to the involuntary killing of a patient, since a death which has not been wished for by that patient can never be considered to be good for that individual. The irreversibility and finality of death are sometimes given scant regard by those who argue about euthanasia for others by propounding their own views. It is well recognized by all those who work with patients who are terminally ill that the views of the medically well often change dramatically when they themselves become ill. Arguments are put forward by the medically well on behalf of the medically ill, but sweeping generalizations can impair the autonomy of the ill and subtly prejudice thinking against the ill and disabled, thereby also impairing the ethical principle of justice.

Why ask for euthanasia rather than commit suicide?

Suicide is the voluntary taking of one's own life, i.e. self-killing. In the act of suicide the individual is acting autonomously in effecting their wish to die; this does not impinge directly on the autonomy of others, as this is a self-act and does not require another person to be the killer. The arguments about assisted suicide are often carried to extremes; anyone who has supplied to a person the means to commit suicide could be argued to be an accessory to the act. The doctor who prescribes powerful drugs with the intention of relieving symptoms, not with the intention of killing the patient, cannot reasonably be deemed to be an assistant if that patient decides to take an overdose of the drugs. Many people are aware of the dangers of paracetamol overdose, and these dangers are clearly printed on supplies of paracetamol which can be purchased over the counter. However, the manufacturers of the drug are not assisting suicide by producing the analgesic, even though there are deaths each year directly attributable to paracetamol overdose.

Therefore, the only people who might be reasonably expected to ask for euthanasia rather than commit suicide when they feel suicidal are those who are physically unable to take their own life, such as those with a stable disability like a quadriplegia, or those who are too ill and weak to take an overdose of a drug. Patients who are too ill and weak to take an overdose are usually within the last hours of life anyway, and therefore death will come as rapidly by natural causes as by the patient contriving to die. There have occasionally been suicides amongst very frail terminally ill patients who have taken a drug overdose, but it is remarkable that many thousands of patients every day are terminally ill and have easy access to extremely powerful drugs but choose not to take them in overdose. The number of patients who physically are totally dependent, such as the quadriplegic, are extremely small. Sadly, their disability has sometimes resulted from the imposition of futile resuscitative procedures, where treatments have been given to the patient without adequate discussion in respect of patient autonomy and without true informed consent.

When a patient asks for euthanasia, it may be that that patient is asking for a response other than a lethal injection. It may be that the patient's physician has removed any hope of symptom control and dignity, but the patient desperately seeks confirmation of personal worth, or the hope of improved quality of life. The way the physician responds has implications for the patient.

How can we respond to a patient who requests euthanasia?

The response of the physician to such a request will have a major influence on the patient's perception of the future. If a physician feels hopeless or unmotivated to care for the patient, the patient's self-perception will be one of worthlessness. The physician who is faced with an intractable clinical problem and feels he has failed in his management of a patient, may find it difficult to overcome personal pride in seeking help from others. However, the patient may not be aware of these personal issues within the physician, and may feel that the statement 'there is nothing more that can be done' is based on an absolute medical truth rather than meaning 'I don't think there is any more I can do for you, but somebody else may be able to do something'. Unwillingness of the physician to refer patients to other colleagues does not allow the patient to enjoy the justice of the right to the best possible treatment in resources available. Thus the physician's pride obstructs the right of a patient to adequate information, and therefore the patient's autonomy is not respected. It is not difficult to envisage instances where it is easier for a physician to dispose of a difficult clinical problem through euthanasia rather than spend time and effort to work through, learn from others and risk exposing his or her own failings.

An alternative response to the patient who requests euthanasia is to recognize this request as a serious cry for help and a statement of despair. Careful history-taking will expose the problems which make the patient's current situation intolerable, and careful analysis of these problems will allow solutions to the individual parts to be obtained. Thus the patient's request for euthanasia is a cry for help and is asking the physician to take their suffering more seriously and to redouble efforts to relieve distress. No one person can have all the answers, but advice sought from colleagues and a multi-disciplinary team approach can be extremely rewarding for the physician humble enough to admit to his or her own deficiencies. All efforts at symptom control must aim to maximize the patient's dignity, minimize dependency and reaffirm the patient's personal worth and value as an individual. This approach has been adopted in hospice care throughout Great Britain, and the experience of those working in hospices is that requests for euthanasia do not persist; reassessment of patients' perception of their quality of life after good palliative care demonstrates improvement.

It is very common for people who suddenly face tragedy to feel that life is not worth living. Thus the patient who suddenly became paraplegic, an event which she had feared more than anything else throughout her life, felt that she had no dignity or personal worth and only wished to die. However, within a short time of good symptom control, effective physiotherapy and occupational therapy to help her adapt to wheelchair living, this same patient spontaneously stated that she never believed life could have so much quality again and that she was getting enjoyment out of things that she had never even previously noticed, such as the intense beauty of the flowers in spring. Readjustment of her role was important to her sense of personal worth.

Is symptom control passive euthanasia?

Euthanasia, where the intention is to kill the patient, is fundamentally different from symptom control. Of course, any medical intervention involves risk, but, as explained above, this risk should always be less than the predicted benefit. With many drugs used in symptom control, there is a risk of sedation as a side-effect, which may consequently decrease coughing and increase the risk of a patient developing a chest infection as a final event. The intention to provide good pain control may unfortunately result in a chest infection, but does not carry the intention to kill and is not done with the express intention of giving a chest infection. This 'double effect' of drugs is not euthanasia.

To obtain symptom control the *minimum* effective dose is the right one, so that benefits are maximized and side-effects minimized. To kill a patient, the intentional use of a maximum dose is required. There is no evidence that good symptom control shortens life, and it may often prolong good-quality life as patients do not become exhausted by intractable symptoms such as pain or vomiting.

Thus the intention with which drugs are given is of paramount importance. In palliative care the intention is to provide symptom control and therefore doses are titrated up to find the most effective dose with the minimum side-effects for the patient. This is completely different to the intentional use of a lethal injection.

Dangers in accepting euthanasia

In Holland, an increasingly secular society, the concept of euthanasia has become respectable through the media and is now taken up by the population at large. However, there has been increasing evidence that the use of lethal injections is not confined to those patients repeatedly requesting euthanasia. It has been used when relatives have requested the death, and even where the health-care professions have acted independently without consultation of patient or relatives. Here the health-care economics of patient turnover rates and bed throughput perilously impair a patient's right to care and allow a selfish materialistic approach in society to avoid a duty to care. There is also evidence from Holland that euthanasia has now been used as a way to kill patients whose disease is not inevitably fatal, and indeed whose prognosis with good medical treatment could be deemed to be good. Cases in the literature recently have included a young girl with anorexia nervosa, and a woman with severe depression following bereavement who refused conventional anti-depressant therapy. The Dutch guidelines were designed to be used for the terminally ill only; they have rapidly become more widely interpreted to begin to allow euthanasia on demand. The evidence from Holland suggests that the demand does not always have to come from the patient; i.e. requests for euthanasia are generated by the family, or instigated by the physician without the expressed wish of the patient, so that patient autonomy is not respected. The dangers of this pattern must be heeded by all those who enter into the euthanasia debate, since the 'slippery-slope' argument cannot be consigned to consequentialist pessimism but is a reality, of which there is evidence from the Netherlands.

Euthanasia has become a difficult debate in our society. Mencken stated that 'for every difficult question, there is an easy answer – short simple and wrong'. The law is and always will be a blunt instrument, and no general regulations can be written for the specifics of an individual. The ethical principles outlined above, and the evidence from those in hospices providing palliative care for patients, clearly demonstrate that there is no need to change the law to permit euthanasia.

The law has a protective function in society and is there to protect the majority of the population. The law protects the individual both from the actions of others and from him- or herself. In every society there are people who would willingly become executioners or torturers, and there are many who secretly enjoy a voyeuristic role when dealing with death and the dying. The law, by prohibiting killing, prevents such people from being able to satisfy their abnormal trait and continues to protect the individual from malpractice by others.

Is withdrawing patient treatment tantamount to euthanasia? Patient autonomy can be easily respected in the competent patient. However, the incompetent patient, rendered unable to communicate, confused or with an impaired level of consciousness, is unable to exercise autonomy. It is for this group of patients that questions of withdrawing treatment usually arise.

There are some important questions which must be asked. Is the treatment of benefit to the patient as a whole person? Treatment which enhances quality of life and personhood of an individual can be deemed to have benefit, whereas treatment which does not enhance the whole sense of a person but simply maintains a 'heart/lung preparation' cannot be deemed beneficial. Similarly, treatment which is burdensome, either to the individual because it is uncomfortable or painful, or causes distress in some other way or is burdensome to society and has no benefit to the patient's overall well-being as a person, can be deemed futile. Such a futile treatment is an 'unjust use' of resources and is meaningless in terms of 'doing good' and 'doing no harm', since the harmful effect is the burdensomeness of the treatment, and the treatment does no good if it is futile. Thus the withdrawal of such a treatment is the cessation of a futile treatment; it may be that as a result of withdrawal of a futile treatment the patient's inevitable death then occurs. However, here again the intention with which the decision was taken is of paramount importance. If a treatment is deliberately withdrawn with the express intention of killing a patient, e.g. if a ventilator is switched off in somebody whose recovery is possible, then the action of withdrawing the treatment is wilful, premeditated killing and defined as murder. If a ventilator is switched off in a patient because the ventilation of the patient is futile and there is no chance of recovery from that situation, then the cessation of treatment is justified, since continuing ventilation of the patient would bring no benefit to the patient as a person and damages other patients by unfairly allocating resources. When such a decision to cease futile treatment is taken, it is important that the patient is not allowed to experience adverse side-effects in the process. Thus measures aimed at control of symptoms and maintenance of patient comfort must be continued.

Arguments over nutrition have been used in this respect. When nutrition is withheld from somebody, that person will starve to death, and therefore nutrition is part of a basic aspect of human care, especially towards a child or any other dependent. In the normal sense, nutrition is not distinctly a medical act. When conventional nutrition is impossible, the maintenance of a patient's nutritional status may become a medical act. At this point the benefit must be weighed up against the risk and burden; parenteral feeding is required for patients whose quality of life and personal worth are maintained by the treatment, but is not indicated in patients in whom such attempts are futile because of the rate of their disease progression. There can be indications to provide nutrition over and above any other medical intervention, even in patients *in extremis*, since there is evidence that adequate nutrition prevents problems such as pressure sores, which are distressing, from occurring.

Decisions to withhold or withdraw medical treatment must be taken based on the four principles outlined at the beginning of this chapter. They are not variations of euthanasia. The term 'passive euthanasia' is a misnomer; it is the intention with which a clinical decision is taken that is of prime importance.

10 The House of Lords Select Committee report

In 1983 a parliamentary inquiry was set up to examine ethical issues surrounding death. This was established as a Select Committee from the House of Lords, under the chairmanship of Lord Walton of Detchant. This committee was the House of Lords Select Committee on Medical Ethics, drawn from peers of widely differing persuasions, and carefully established as a balanced committee. The committee was appointed to consider the ethical, legal and clinical implications of a person's right to withhold consent to life-prolonging treatment, and the position of persons who are no longer able to give or withhold consent; also to consider whether in what circumstances actions that have as their intention the likely consequence of the shortening of another person's life may be justified on the grounds that they accord with that person's wishes or with that person's best interest, and in all the foregoing considerations to pay regard to the likely effects of changes in law or medical practice on society as a whole. The committee took evidence widely from many people including those in favour of euthanasia, professional groups involved in the care of patients and patient representatives. They also took individual submissions of evidence, and no evidence was refused. The committee visited Holland and took evidence there in the light of Dutch attitudes to euthanasia.

The report of this committee was published on 17 February 1994. It is clearly written and explores all these issues in depth.

It is a valuable document and should be studied by all who profess an interest in medical ethics. It is worth noting that the conclusions of the Select Committee on Medical Ethics include:

- A recommendation that there should be no change in the law to permit euthanasia.
- Strong endorsement of the right of the competent patient to refuse consent to any medical treatment.
- That double effect is not a reason for withholding treatment that would give relief, as long as the doctor acts in accordance with responsible medical practice with the objective of relieving pain or stress and without the intention to kill.
- Treatment decisions should be made by all involved in the care of a patient on the basis that treatment may be judged inappropriate if it would add nothing to the patient's wellbeing as a person.
- It should be unnecessary to consider the withdrawal of nutrition and hydration, except if its administration is in itself burdensome to the patient.
- Treatment-limiting decisions should not be determined by resource availability.
- Long-term care of dependent people should have special regard to maintenance of dignity.
- A change in the law on assisted suicide is not recommended.

For details on these and other conclusions the reader is referred to the report.

11 Conclusion

Clinical palliative care embodies the practice of medical ethics. When the key principles of autonomy, including informed consent, beneficence, non-maleficence and justice are invoked in decision-making, the result is good care which is cost-effective, and improved quality of life for the patients.

Background documents and papers

Association for Palliative Medicine of Great Britain and Ireland,

Southampton. Palliative medicine curriculum; Guidelines for teaching palliative medicine (at all grades).

Bluebond-Langner M. *The Private Worlds of Dying Children* (Princeton, Princeton University Press, 1987).

British Medical Association. *Philosophy and Practice of Medical Ethics* (London, BMA, 1988).

Browne, K. and P. Freeling. *The Doctor-Patient Relationship* (Edinburgh and London, Livingstone, 1967).

Report of the Select Committee on Medical Ethics, House of Lords (HL Paper 21 I) (London, HMSO, 1994).

Jeffrey, D. *There is Nothing More I Can Do* (London, The Lisa Sainsbury Foundation, 1993).

Mason, J. K. and R. A. McCall Smith. *Law and Medical Ethics* (London, Dublin and Edinburgh, Butterworth, 1991).

Scott, W. E., M. D. Vickers and H. Draper. *Ethical Issues in Anaesthesia* (London, Butterworth and Heinemann, 1994).

Skegg, P. D. G. *Law, Ethics and Medicine* (Oxford University Press, 1990).

Wilkinson, John. 'Ethical issues in palliative care', in *Oxford Textbook of Palliative Medicine*, ed. E. Doyle, G. W. C. Hanks and N. MacDonald (Oxford University Press, 1993).

6
Pastoral care of the dying and bereaved

HEATHER SNIDLE

1 Introduction

Separation and loss are part of our lives, and we ourselves or
those we work with may well be suffering from them. They can
take many forms – burglary, moving house, changing jobs, stillbirth, miscarriage, the birth of a handicapped child, infertility,
rape, loss of speech, disfigurement, divorce, being faced with
residential care, imprisonment, loss of a pet, redundancy, or as a
result of accident, or death.

Grief is an integral part of normal life, and the strong feelings
it can evoke are a natural response to loss. The baby must leave
the womb, the child its parents on entering school, the adoles-
cent its family to lead an independent life. From babyhood we
learn that crying appears to demand a response and a re-estab-
lishment of human connections, and with maturity comes inner
resources and knowledge, growing independence and self-awareness. We learn that loss is survivable.

Bowlby and others have shown that the quality of attachment
in childhood will influence later behaviour and loss management.[1] If this is not learnt in childhood it can lead to denial of
feeling and withdrawal from relationships in adult life, thus
'protecting' ourselves from pain; loss not acknowledged can lead
to coldness and denial of feelings. Each person's response to loss
is unique – the product of personal experience.

We all live in an uncertain, rapidly changing world in which we
cannot predict the future; the only inescapable certainty is that
we all face death. This one certainty is often too sombre to be
faced openly; yet every time a loved one, colleague or patient
dies, we are reminded vividly of our own death. This can force us

to face fundamental questions.

Caring for the dying and bereaved is a challenge for professionals. It means trying to understand, listening attentively, being sensitive enough to understand what is not said, and remembering that they still need to be needed, and to feel there is still a purpose to life. Care must take into consideration all aspects, the physical, social, cultural, psychological and emotional, spiritual and religious needs of both the dying and the bereaved.

Good communication and trust are vital. A conspiracy of silence is damaging to all. Mutual trust is the basic building block of care, the patient and their loved ones must trust the professionals' competence, and trust each other, and all must work together for the good of all concerned. Anticipated death gives people a chance to come to terms with dying, to plan for the remaining future, to put life in order, to say goodbye. It allows loved ones to start the grieving process; sudden death denies this opportunity.

2 Caring for the dying

Anticipated death has many facets, and people have to come to terms with these in their owntime, and in their own way. Death and dying are not the same; dying is a process; death can be seen as the point in time when life ceases, or death can mean the time after this point, and how people approach this will depend on their religious and personal beliefs. People may be afraid of one aspect but not another, or worry about different aspects at different points in time.

Care of the dying also involves caring for their loved ones. The family members – parents, grandparents and siblings, as well as other loved ones, suffer from shock, depression and anxiety, in much the same way as the terminally ill person does, and they may also share many of the same fears. They too have to come to terms with the disease and its impact and unfamiliar demands on them. These people, like the patient, also need help to express their feelings of pain, anger, grief and fear. They may need help to mobilize their strengths and capacities to deal with the situation. They therefore need acceptance, help and support themselves, much the same information, and an opportunity to talk things through. Talking things through will help in the realization that others share feelings, experiences and understanding. It helps put things into a clearer perspective. It gives a chance to moan and cry, to express pain, anger and grief and not feel guilty. It will also help mobilize inner strength.

Patients, families and partners all need to talk to someone trusted; and help to cope with the patient/loved ones; to cope with their own suffering, and to cope with their own feeling about illness, disability, disfigurement, death and dying. In both the patient and their loved ones, the physical, psychological, emotional, spiritual and social effects will ebb and flow, lasting for hours or days.

It is traumatic for any family to be told that their loved one , in the prime of life, has a terminal disease. How much worse to be told your child/loved one has a socially unacceptable disease, e.g. Aids. Parents may now learn that their child took drugs or is gay, or a partner may now learn that their partner took drugs or was bisexual. Their reaction may be one of anger, shame, guilt and fear, and this may lead them to reject the child/partner, or treat him/her as a 'leper'. They too may feel like social outcasts. This double adjustment in coping with homosexuality/bisexuality/ drug-taking and terminal illness can create an immense conflict and trauma. Often many parents may suspect their son is gay but deny it, so that they also have the psychological pain caused by the loss of this defence. Yet often, when the extended family is told, it is discovered that they already know about the homosexuality and would have been more supportive to the parents had there not been this conspiracy of silence.

In any terminal illness parents may resent the partner, and partners in turn may resent the parents. Either may feel isolated, and this is often compounded by feelings of remorse, grief and guilt. They may worry about who will look after them if they also become ill. This can make the future appear very lonely and threatening. It must also be remembered that elderly carers who are caring for adult children, or grandchildren whose parents are ill or have died, can be unwell themselves, and this can put an added pressure on them.

Loved ones have to understand and care for their own needs if they are to be able to help their patient. This is not something many of us can do alone. Realizing that others share your feelings and experiences begins to put things into a clearer perspective. The family may also need help with communication; if the family have frequent help to ventilate their feelings, it may make a big difference to each individual's ability to cope. There is often a sense of loss and meaninglessness, and for some there is despair about the future. They may require a great deal of help, understanding, support and acceptance.

Parents of a terminally ill child often feel they cannot admit the problem even to themselves, and are often very reluctant to inform their children of their situation, and may need help and support to do this. The uncertain progression of disease can be difficult to explain. Will the child cope with the stress of this? The child has a right to know the results of tests – it is his or her illness. Rational thought and explanation may not be enough, the child may become upset, and behavioural problems may result. Children may blame the mother or father and sever a main source of support. How emotionally capable are they to accept this? It is often adults that find this difficult. What counselling will be required? Even young children need acceptance of facts and help to write a will. The emphasis should be on the quality of life and its enjoyment, and on funerals as a celebration of life.

It has been observed that in some families the ill child does well, but other children are neglected because all the attention is going to the ill child. Living with uncertainty about the course of the disease can lead to extreme anxiety, hospital visits can be traumatic, and this can be compounded by the mother's tiredness as ill health makes increasing demands on her. Women are usually the principal carers. How will they cope with their anxieties? Will statutory services be flexible and responsive? Will family and friends be supportive?

Siblings also need support, however, and overprotection can be a major problem. Older children may also need help to cope with their feelings about their own death.

It is important to remember that ill children have the same needs as other children – for play and stimulation, for friendship and affection. They need hugging and cuddling. Alternative care may be required as an emergency, planned or respite care. This is very important for a mother, especially if she or another member of the family is also ill.

Parents who may be very supportive of their child's illness and a 'tower of strength' may collapse at its death when they no longer have to be strong.

3 Grief as a process

Grief is not an illness, but a natural process that must be allowed to run its course; and this takes *time*. Each person will have to establish their *own* method of recovery. There is *no* right or wrong way to grieve. There is, however, a pattern to the resolution of grief, and there is help available. People are often frightened by the intensity and variety of feelings they may experience. No one can resolve grief for another; resolution can be gained only by experiencing and working through these emotions. Pain may become less intense but is seldom forgotten; memories can trigger periods of intense pain long after the event.

Bereavement may not be an isolated loss but an additional burden. The process of bereavement may depend on the individual's perception of the situation and perceived ability to cope with it and discharge emotional tensions caused by stress. Worden sees the tasks of grieving as recognizing the loss, releasing the various emotions, developing new skills and reinvesting emotional energy.[2] For most people grief has no predecessor, its path cannot be anticipated. Grief, Staudacher reminds us, is a process, with stages that can be moved between or experienced simultaneously.[3] Yet it is something that cannot be circumvented, but must be faced in order to continue life in a meaningful way.

Grief is an essential element of life, it is the process of becoming re-anchored into a life without the husband, wife, partner, relative or friend for whom one is grieving. This can begin with anticipation of the death, days, months or even years before.

Watching a loved one die and the period following death can be a lonely experience. Feelings of isolation can be caused by seclusion from normal life, pain, physical distance and the prior death or absence of loved ones. This can arouse very strong emotions, feelings of anger, sorrow, failure or guilt, some of which can be deeply buried in the subconscious. Those watching may deny reality or bargain for life to continue. They may be in the deep depression of preparatory grief or have begun to accept the prognosis and be trying to live on a very difficult day-to-day process.

Grief is painful, and the loss affects many aspects of a person's life, not just feelings about the lost person, but also intellectual processes, interpersonal relations, beliefs, attitudes, emotions and physical health. In order to help manage loss, people need others who can offer complete and unconditional acceptance, empathic understanding and congruence. When someone loses a loved one, it is not one loss but many, a death of a spouse may mean loss of a companion, helpmate, mother or father to the children, breadwinner, sexual partner, car driver, do-it-yourself expert, cook etc.

The symptoms of normal grief are:

painful dejection
loss of interest in the outside world
temporary loss of the capacity to love
physical distress
preoccupation with the dead person
feelings of guilt towards the deceased
hostile feelings to others
altered conduct.

The above are *normal* symptoms of acute grief and the only way to resolve them is to work through them. The pain of grief cannot be avoided healthily. Delayed, suppressed or distorted grief can cause problems in later years.

Parkes found four phases associated with grief:[4]

(1) Numbness, where the predominant feelings are shock and disbelief.
(2) Yearning, where the predominant feelings are reminiscence, searching, hallucinations, anger and guilt.
(3) Disorganization and despair, where the predominant feelings are anxiety, loneliness, ambivalence, fear, hopelessness and helplessness.
(4) Reorganization, where the predominant feelings are of acceptance and relief.

These phases overlap, and we move between them in our own unique way.

Parkes's research shows that the outcome of grief is affected by 'determinants' of grief, some of which can make grief more complicated and prolonged. These 'determinants' can be both external circumstances and internal factors.

Worden summarizes these 'determinants' as external and internal factors.[5]

4 External factors

(1) The place of death, for example if someone dies far away or is missing, presumed dead, this can lead to the postponement of grief or it can inhibit it altogether.
(2) Coincidental deaths, for example following an accident, where more than one person is killed. Here each person needs to be individually grieved for, or where there is a major community loss e.g. following a community disaster, which makes grieving far more complex, and where less comfort and support may be available.
(3) Successive deaths, when another loss occurs before grief is complete.
(4) The nature of the death – untimely death is more difficult to grieve, and sudden death can be traumatic, especially following a disaster, suicide or homicide. This can be complicated by extreme guilt at the failure to save the victim. Such anger is hard to express.
(5) Social networks are important, social isolation and lack of support prolong grief.

5 Internal factors.

(1) Attachment history: a previous loss can be reawakened.
(2) Loss and death history.
(3) Age and development of the griever: at certain vulnerable points in the life cycle grief may be especially challenging.
(4) The more intimate the attachment, the more intense the grief.
(5) The more complex the relationship the more complex the grief. Denied feelings and unrecognized ambivalence make grief complex.
(6) If the griever has and can use a religious faith, this can give consolation.

Anger is often a new reality, and a logical and natural part of grieving. The direction anger will take will depend on the situation, personality and gender. It may be anger at God, anger at the unfairness of the world, anger directed at self or at others or even towards the deceased. In addition to anger, guilt can hit without warning.

Grief can also be physical; heart palpitations, loss of appetite, overeating, ringing in the ears, digestive problems, nausea, dizziness, nightmares, interrupted sleep, lethargy, constriction in the throat, muscular pains, impeded concentration, poor memory, damp hands, dry mouth and insomnia are common symptoms found in grief. Grief also causes feelings of helplessness, anger, preoccupation with the deceased, a sense of presence, visual and auditory hallucinations, restlessness, apathy, shock, numbness, forgetfulness, disbelief, sadness, crying, meaninglessness, despair, loneliness, social withdrawal, confusion and lethargy. These manifestations are the same as those found in states of fear or anxiety. This is clearly explained by C. S. Lewis: 'No one ever told me that grief felt so like fear. I am not afraid, but the sensation is like being afraid.'[6]

Death in our society is often 'hidden'. In earlier centuries death was more 'present' and less 'banished' from our midst. This process has been accompanied by an increased denial of death, and fear of it.

The process of grief is unique to each individual and depends on the deceased's journey in and through life, the circumstances of the death, the relationship, the mourner's own present circumstances and life history; these are unique to each individual.

6   Sex role differences

Lendrum and Syne remind us that we are also affected by sex role differences, as 'men seem to need to regain control of their world more quickly, are more immediately in touch with intense sexual feeling and are also aware of the threat to sexuality which loss of a partner can pose . . . Men find it difficult to express the sadness of grief and in most cultures it is the women who do the wailing.'[7] However, both sexes have a basically similar underlying pattern of response to grief.

7 Death of a child

When a baby or child dies unexpectedly the shock can be immense. Parents may go over what happened repeatedly, and wonder if they could somehow have prevented the death. They may blame themselves, each other or other professionals; or they may feel very guilty. These are natural responses even when the child's death was outside their control. These feelings of blame and guilt are often shared by other members of the family as well, and by professionals, for example childminders, foster-parents, doctors, health visitors and social workers who may have had responsibility for the child.

Caring for parents who have lost a baby or small child is demanding and stressful work. Kohner and Henley believe that the parents' ability to grieve and eventually to accept their loss is largely dependent on their experience of professional care.[8]

8 Grief in childhood

Discussing and explaining death to children in the family is a very difficult task and can be even more distressing when parents are in the midst of their own grief. They may try to 'protect' the children from discussion of death and leave them out of the rituals associated with death. This can leave children feeling anxious, bewildered and alone at a time when they most need help and reassurance.

Children who may not fully understand need love and accep-tance from the significant people in their lives to help them maintain their own security. Children too young to verbalize their feelings may express them through behaviour and play. It is very important to remember that, regardless of their ability or inability to express themselves, children do grieve, often very deeply. Their grief process is similar to that of adults, but they may also fear that they too may die, or they may feel left out, or fear that they somehow caused the death, or that the significant people in their life may also die. These fears can lead to regres-sion, to behaviour previously outgrown.

It is very important to answer children's questions honestly, to allow them to express themselves, and not to tell a child what he should feel. Lies and euphemisms complicate children's grief.

They know they are not getting the whole truth, and this leads to mistrust at a time when reassurance is most required. It is important to try and explain the cause of death and to explain the associated rituals. It is very important to be loving, accepting, truthful and consistent. How well children cope with bereavement depends on many factors including their age, the characteristics of the dead person, sibling order, and above all the reactions and availability of the significant others in their life.

Children will be affected by death in ways depending on their developmental stage. A baby will be affected by the parents' emotional state and may miss the deceased. They may have sleeping problems and weight loss, and appear very unsettled. Toddlers do not understand the permanence of death, nor do they easily distinguish between fact and fantasy. They may wonder what they did wrong, or suffer from separation anxiety.

Three- to seven-year-olds may act out the loss in play, and ask questions without real understanding, which can be confusing for parents. They will often try to comfort parents in ways they had been previously comforted. They may search for the lost one, and/or become fearful that they or their parents may die, and become afraid to let them out of their sight.

Seven- to twelve-year-olds think concretely and have little ability to deal with subtleties, ambiguities or euphemisms, so care must be taken not to say, 'We lost Fred' or 'Grandpa has gone to sleep', or they may be afraid of being lost or going to sleep. At about ten years of age the irreversibility of death begins to be grasped, and they realize that they too will die one day. Over this age a child perceives the finality of death much as an adult does. The understanding of death is age-related but *not* age-specific.

Unresolved grief in adulthood can frequently be attributed to a serious childhood loss. Parents may be unable to help each other, let alone a child, because they are locked in their own pain. Members of the family may need help both together and separately. Family members may need help to recognize that they may all grieve differently.

9   Faith in grief

Most people turn to their relatives and friends for comfort; some will turn to their faith for support. Faith may be or become important at this time. Often the long-ignored faith of childhood takes on a new significance. For people of many different faiths, this can be a source of strength and comfort. For the Christian, Jew and Muslim, death is a gateway, a new beginning, a fulfilment of human life; and at our final unknown destination total fulfilment is to be found. For many, then, death is not something to fear but to welcome.

Basil Hume reminds us that words like 'hope', 'expectation' and 'looking forward' are important in the evening of life; at this time people look forward to the vision of God. This will vary with different religious groups. For many it may well be the ecstasy of love which is union with God. Hume, writing about Christianity, reminds us that 'This should be a cause of peace, a cause of joy; one day forward, one step nearer.' This may also hold for other religious groups, however God is defined.[9]

10 Rituals

Rituals associated with death are very important and vary widely with different ethnic and religious groups, and also within groups. Rituals help force people to confront the reality of a loss, and enable those who are grieving to come together to express their grief supported by the community. Rites communicate to the community the new status and role of the surviving partner, they provide emotional release and offer an opportunity for the loss and associated emotions to be dealt with. They link our individual experience with the corporate experience of the community.

Each culture has its own mourning rites and ways of handling death. These may be intended for the dead, but they also fulfil functions for the living, helping the bereaved to recognize the loss and providing a place for the expression of grief publicly in a prescribed way. These also help to mark a transition, helping to say goodbye. Rituals in different cultures also help to limit mourning. It is important for us to develop a sensitivity to different requirements of faith in our multicultural society.

Within the Christian faith, most denominations have accommodated to contemporary practices, though some still refuse cremation. Some sects will not accept certain medical procedures such as blood transfusion or a post-mortem. Catholics and some Anglicans will expect to be given extreme unction, and perhaps celebrate the Eucharist. This can be very important to both the dying and to their families.

In the Jewish faith death must be resisted, and believers always hope that this is not the end. At the point of death, the rabbi will read the deathbed confession over the dying person which carries the promise that life may continue. In an orthodox family, as the person is dying, the nearest relatives will want to be present to say certain psalms and, finally, the *Shema* (or basic law). The body is sacred and must be laid out properly by members of the same sex. The immediate family members conduct and are at the centre of the mourning ritual, which starts immediately on death. Once death has occurred, there are other sacred demands. The first seven days (*shiva*) are the most intense period of grief, and the next thirty days mark a period of lesser mourning. After a year a stone is set at the grave, and the bereaved may let go of their grief and remarry if they are ready.

Muslims are enjoined to prepare for death as a proper end to life, through living a pious life. Death is not to be feared in living out God's will. Indeed it can be welcomed if it comes in the pursuit of God's commands. As death approaches, debts should be paid, enemies forgiven, reconciliation sought and a will made. The body is then prepared in readiness for death, by tidying the hair, washing and reciting the Qur'ān and by prayers. To keep the devil away, the Kalima is recited aloud. After death the body is ritually washed and prepared for burial. Non-Muslims should remember never to touch the body of a dead Muslim unless wearing gloves. Burial is within twenty-four hours, and mourning lasts forty days. As death is not a disaster, grief should be subdued or triumphant.

For Hindus and Sikhs death must not come unawares. It is important, therefore, to be open with the terminally ill person and their family. Family and other members of the community should be present to prepare the dying person for death. This can include reading or chanting scripture, and other acts of devotion, including burning incense, sprinkling the patient with holy water and giving food and drink. Hindus seek to die on the floor. On death, further lamentations and rituals are performed. These can be very disturbing and misunderstood in a public institution. Hindu religious practices vary enormously. The body should not be touched by a non-Hindu, and cremation should be done on the day of death or as soon as possible. The thirteenth day marks the end of official mourning.

When a Sikh dies the family lay the body out and ensure the five signs of Sikhism are worn. Cremation is mandatory and should be as soon as possible. Official mourning lasts for ten days.

Different cultural and racial backgrounds must always be considered, and a knowledge of beliefs about death, afterlife and mourning practices in different religious and cultural groups is essential in our multi-racial, multi-ethnic and multi-belief society.

11 Helping someone who is bereaved

Helping someone who is bereaved is often more to do with 'being' than 'doing'. The bereaved need to be able to share their inner feelings, to talk and to grapple with the 'why'. Listening should be with acceptance, understanding and empathy, allowing grievers to find their own words. It is important to indicate understanding of the feelings expressed and to be able to link them with experience and behaviour, and so to help the expression and acknowledgement of feelings. Offering clear boundaries gives safety and containment, which is important in encouraging expression and acceptance of feelings, ambivalence and guilt. This demands sensitivity and self-awareness.

Shock may mean that information needs to be repeated, and the same issues may need repeated discussion as bereavement may make the absorption of information difficult. Denial of feelings may lead to depression, and a greater inability to absorb the information given.

Professionals are likely to be able to offer better support for bereaved people if they themselves are supported. This support should include provision to share their experiences and feelings, supportive management and teamwork, as well as basic and in-service training on bereavement and the essential skills needed to help bereaved people.

Death needs a holistic approach, remembering each person is unique, and should be considered as a whole, taking account of the physical, emotional, psychological, social and spiritual

dimensions. A balance must be maintained between acknow-
ledging the loss and trying at the same time to maintain a positive
perspective. It is important to talk of the loss, and of the value of
the person who died, about how he or she enriched the lives of
others, and to look to the positive in the future.

Help can come from many sources, from family, friends, faith,
support groups or professionals. Complicated grief may need
professional help. In making a referral for professional help, feelings of guilt, anger or rejection need to be recognized, accepted
and worked through.

Notes

1. See J. Bowlby, *Attachment and Loss* (Harmondsworth, Penguin, 1980).
2. J. W. Worden, *Grief Counselling and Grief Therapy* (London, Tavistock, 1983).
3. C. Staudacher, *Beyond Grief: A Guide for Recovering from the Death of a Loved One* (London, Condor Books, 1987).
4. C. M. Parkes, *Bereavement: Studies of Grief in Adult Life* (Harmondsworth, Penguin, 1985).
5. Worden, *Grief Counselling.*
6. C. S. Lewis, *A Grief Observed* (London, Faber, 1961).
7. S. Lendrum and G. Syne, *Gift of Tears: A Practical Approach to Loss and Bereavement Counselling* (London, Routledge, 1992), 30.
8. N. Kohner and A. Henley, 'Miscarriage, stillbirth and neonatal death', in *Guide Lines for the Professionals* (London, SANDS, 1991).
9. B. Hume, *To Be a Pilgrim* (London, St Paul Publications/SPCK, 1984), 226.

Sources of support

The Compassionate Friends, National Secretary, 6 Denmark Street,
Bristol BS1 5QD (telephone 0117 9 292778).
Cruse (the national organization for the widowed and their children),
126 Sheen Road, Richmond TW9 1UR (telephone 0171 940
4818/9407).
The Foundation for the Study of Infant Deaths; Cot Death Research
and Support, 15 Belgrave Square, London SW1X 8PS (telephone
0171 235 1721).
Gay Bereavement Project, 46 Wentworth Road, London NW11 0RL.

7
A theological examination of the case for euthanasia

PAUL BADHAM

1 The strength of the tradition against euthanasia

All the mainstream churches are resolutely opposed to the practice of euthanasia and to any change in the law which would
make it more likely to occur. This may be illustrated both in the
evidence submitted by Christian bodies to the House of Lords
Committee on Medical Ethics,[1] and in the uncompromising
declaration of the latest Catholic catechism. According to this
catechism promulgated by Pope John Paul II in 1992 and
published in English in 1994,

> An act or omission which, of itself or by intention, causes death in
> order to eliminate suffering constitutes a murder gravely contrary to
> the dignity of the human person and to the respect due to the living
> God, his Creator. The error of judgement into which one can fall in
> good faith does not change the nature of this murderous act, which
> must always be forbidden and excluded.[2]

For many Christians therefore the question of euthanasia is a
non-issue. It is something their tradition has always forbidden
and their leaders continue to oppose. Catholics and Evangelicals
are united on this matter. For the vast majority of members of
both Christian traditions euthanasia is simply wrong. Insofar as
being a Christian includes being a member of a community of
faith and sharing in its moral ethos, it would seem to many
Christians that the issue is closed.

2   The relevance of religious factors in the current debate

Many Christians feel strengthened in their principled stand against euthanasia by the fact that euthanasia is strongly supported by the British Humanist Association. Indeed the evidence of that association to the House of Lords pleaded the case for allowing euthanasia on the grounds that an absolutist stance on the sanctity of human life 'depended on a religious outlook which not everyone shared' and urged, 'it is particularly hurtful to require someone who does not believe in God or after-life to suffer intolerable pain or indignity in deference to a God or afterlife he does not accept.'[3] In fact the House of Lords Committee 'gave much thought' to the consideration that 'for those without religious belief, the individual is best able to decide what manner of death is fitting to the life which has been lived.'[4] By implication, therefore, the Select Committee recognized that they were dealing with a situation where there was a significant divide between the views of religious people on the one hand and those of secularists on the other, and they recognized their duty to try and prevent this fact from blurring the impartiality required of them as a body seeking to act on behalf of the community as a whole.

However the fact that division of opinion about euthanasia tends to follow differences of opinion about matters of religious belief is an important consideration which needs to be brought into the current debate. Characteristically euthanasia is debated as either a medical or a philosophical issue. On the medical front, proponents of euthanasia claim that the sufferings endured by at least some terminally ill people could justify the legalization of voluntary euthanasia. By contrast, opponents of euthanasia argue that good medical practice can alleviate such suffering in other ways, and that the trust between doctor and patient requires a continued ban on such so-called 'mercy-killing'. On the philo-sophical front, the debate tends to focus on issues of human rights and personal autonomy weighed against the needs of society as a whole.

Yet although these are the terms in which the issue is publicly debated, the way people evaluate the various considerations depends for the most part on their religious outlook. The bishops and the members of the British Humanist Society both have access to the same medical information and to the philosophical, social and legal considerations adduced by both sides in the euthanasia debate. The divide actually comes on the theological view that euthanasia infringes the prerogatives of God, who alone has the right to determine the hour of our death. It is the validity of this consideration which ought to be questioned and the purpose of this chapter is to do just that.

3   Changing attitudes in Christian ethics

Although many Christians tend to assume that their beliefs are absolute and unchanging, this is not the case. Many things that Christians of a former age believed to be morally acceptable are now held to be wrong and vice versa. Slavery is the classic example of something formerly regarded as acceptable but now regarded with abhorrence. By contrast, the acceptability of interest charges is an example of something totally condemned by one age but seen as morally neutral in another. However, medical ethics provides the largest number of instances where Christians today almost unanimously accept as good, practices which their predecessors in the faith regarded as evil. For many centuries Christians forbade the giving of medicine, deeming it equivalent to the practice of sorcery.[5] The practice of surgery, the study of anatomy and the dissection of corpses for medical research were all at one time firmly forbidden.[6] Later the practices of inoculation and vaccination faced fierce theological opposition. Indeed in 1829 Pope Leo XII declared that whoever decided to be vaccinated was no longer a child of God; smallpox was a judgement of God, vaccination was a challenge to heaven.[7] For similar reasons the initial use of quinine against malaria was denounced by many Christians.[8]   The introduction of anaesthesia and, above all, the use of chloroform in childbirth were seen as directly challenging the biblical judgement that, because of their inheritance of the guilt of Eve's original sin, all women must face the penalty that 'in pain you shall bring forth children'.[9] Consequently the use of chloroform in childbirth was vigorously attacked from public pulpits throughout Britain and the United States,[10] and Queen Victoria's acceptance of such treatment was profoundly controversial.

The root objection to all the medical practices mentioned above was the belief that the duty of human beings was to submit in patience to what God had willed. All innovations in medical practice were initially seen as implying a lack of faith and trust in God's good purposes. Doctors were accused of 'playing God', of being unwilling to accept that God knows what is right for a particular person, of prying into sacred mysteries and areas of God's own prerogative.[11] Yet gradually all mainstream Christian churches have modified their teaching, and the formerly criticized activity of the doctor has itself come to be seen as itself a channel of God's love and the vehicle of his providence. Consequently although the practice of medicine faced opposition in earlier centuries, a very close relationship now often exists between doctors and clergy, and medically-trained missionaries have made a substantial contribution to the worldwide diffusion of Western medicine. Christians today are happy to think of doctors as fulfilling the will of God in restoring to health persons struck down by curable illness. Instead of their actions being seen as challenging divine providence they are seen as agents of that providence.

The salient point for our present purposes however is to note that the same arguments were used in the past against the use of medicine to postpone death as are used today against the use of medicine to bring death forward in the case of terminal illness. In both instances the key religious argument was the belief classically expressed by Aquinas, that 'God alone has authority to decide about life and death.'[12] The human obligation is simply to accept and abide by the will of God in such matters. But one implication of this is that the Christian churches today are being wholly inconsistent in continuing with an absolute stand against euthanasia while enthusiastically supporting medical efforts to fight disease. The change which has taken place in the understanding of divine providence as it affects the acceptability of fighting disease has equal application to the possibility of accepting the practice of euthanasia. Hence I suggest that it is legitimate for a theologian to look more closely at the arguments against euthanasia and reconsider its possible acceptability to the Christian conscience.

4 A definition of voluntary euthanasia

The understanding of euthanasia which I am working with in this chapter is euthanasia as assisted suicide in the context of terminal illness. The essence of the voluntary euthanasia campaign is the idea that a free, autonomous person should have the right both to choose when the struggle against terminal illness should be abandoned, and also, if the process of dying entails suffering of a kind he or she does not wish to endure, the possibility of obtaining assistance in bringing the process to an end without the collaborator facing a murder charge. It is important to stress that one is not seeking a 'right' to die, such as would overide the equally important autonomy of the doctor. No one should be saddled with a duty to kill someone who asks for death, and many requests for euthanasia will continue as now to be expressions of a longing for the relief of pain or suffering, to which the provision of better palliative care will often be a better response than acceding to the request. Nevertheless the supporters of voluntary euthanasia believe that there are cases where a person may request help in dying, and where the person appealed to would be morally justified if he or she were willing to accede to such a request. I have explored the problems of defining such cases elsewhere.[13] In this chapter I am assuming that there are at least some cases where euthanasia as assisted suicide could be morally justified, and am then arguing that this is a position which a committed Christian believer could accept.

5 The Bible's attitude to suicide

One of the main sources of Christian morality is the teaching of the Bible. In most discussions of suicide or euthanasia, Christians tend to assume that the canon of scripture forbids such practices. But it is actually Shakespeare speaking through Hamlet who declared that 'The Everlasting [has] . . . fixed his canon gainst self-slaughter.' And therefore according to Hamlet the 'calamity of so long life' must be endured and we must 'rather bear those ills we have, than fly to others that we know not of.'[14] It is not the case that the canonical scriptures actually forbid suicide. They forbid murder, and hence perhaps, by implication, suicide, but the implication is not spelt out, and suicides are recorded in the Bible without condemnation. Let me quickly illustrate this by running through them. Samson is said to have been given strength by God to pull the house of Dagon down upon his own head so that he would die with his enemies.[15] The suicides of King Saul and his armour-bearer in order to escape the humiliation of capture and mockery are reported without any negative comment, and their deaths were lamented by the whole of Israel.[16] Eleazur Avaran is said to have 'given his life to save his people and to win himself an everlasting name' by stabbing a war elephant from beneath so that it fell on him and killed him as well as the enemies whom it carried.[17] Razis 'fell upon his own sword, preferring to die nobly than to fall into the hands of sinners and suffer outrages unworthy of his noble birth.'[18] In none of these cases is there any hint of disapproval. In the New Testament we are of course told that Judas Iscariot hanged himself, but this is simply reported without comment.[19] The woe predicated on Judas was prior to the suicide, not consequential upon it.[20] The overall picture of the biblical suicides might suggest that the kamikaze deeds of Samson and Eleazur were praiseworthy and the 'death before dishonour' attitude of Saul and Razis was commendable.

6   Biblical attitudes to the willing surrender of life

For Christians, the foundation for ethical behaviour is the imitation of Christ. Historically he died a cruel death at the hands of his enemies. Yet strangely the fourth Gospel presents it as the product of Jesus' own choice to lay down his life: 'No one takes it from me, I lay it down of my own accord.'[21] In one of Jesus' best-loved parabolic images, he pictures himself as a good shepherd ready to lay down his life for his sheep, and what is often overlooked is that the imagery makes no sense except on the supposition that a caring shepherd might be willing to make such a choice.[22] Jesus also taught that a readiness to die for another is the ultimate true test of friendship, 'Greater love has no man than this that a man lay down his life for his friends.'[23] Such a saying may not be strictly relevant to a discussion of suicide, though it is interesting to recall that these verses came into the mind of Scott in the Antarctic when the dying Captain Oates walked out into the snow to perish quickly and thereby enhance the chances of survival for all his colleagues. What such verses suggest is that death is not the ultimate evil to be avoided at all costs. It is something which can be legitimately embraced as a positive good. The sanctity of life is not a biblical absolute. It is a value which has to be balanced against other values.

7 The Christian acceptance of death

Acceptance of death in a positive spirit was for centuries perceived as a normative Christian attitude. St Paul seems consciously to have chosen to go to Jerusalem even though he knew that such a decision would probably lead to his death.[24] Yet he felt no concern about this prospect: 'I am on the point of being sacrificed; the time of my departure has come. I have fought a good fight. I have finished my course. I have kept the faith. Henceforth there is laid up for me a crown of righteousness.'[25] During the centuries of persecution, a willingness to die for the faith was deemed to be one of the supreme Christian virtues. Indeed St Athanasius cited the eagerness with which Christians of his age sought out martyrdom as in itself a proof of the resurrection of Jesus. For Athanasius, it was axiomatic that Christians had no fear whatsoever of death but looked forward to it with joyful anticipation.[26] In the nineteenth century missionaries willingly went out to the 'white man's grave' of malarial West Africa for the sake of the Christian Gospel. Of course willingness to face martyrdom or high risk of disease for the sake of spreading the Gospel are not precisely what is normally meant by suicide, for even though death may have been virtually certain, it was not chosen in itself but was the by-product of other choices. On the other hand, such choices do draw attention to the fact that the Christian tradition does not see death as a fate to be avoided at all costs, but as one which may be legitimately accepted for some sufficient cause.

When we turn more explicitly to the question of whether choosing death might be a legitimate alternative to continuing with life, the most relevant texts would seem to be those which discuss the value of life in the context of terminal illness. Clearly there are abundant verses which speak of the worthwhileness of life when one is enjoying health and vigour. In such circumstances the thought of death is very bitter.[27] But when death comes at the end of a long life the situation is very different: 'O death, how welcome is your sentence to one who is in need and is failing in strength, very old and distracted over everything; to one who is contrary, and has lost his patience!'[28] And if the movement for voluntary euthanasia were looking for a text which summed up their whole perspective it might be Ecclesiasticus 30:17, 'Death is better than a miserable life, and eternal rest than chronic sickness.' My argument is that it is exactly this judgement that a modern Christian should be allowed to make and to act upon in the closing stages of life. From both a biblical perspective and from the perspective of the mainstream Christian tradition, death is not something to be feared, but when it comes in the fullness of time, it is to be welcomed. It is tragic that this dimension is so missing in contemporary Church life that modern hymn books asterisk for suggested omission the verse relating to death in St Francis of Assisi's famous Canticle:

> And thou, most kind and gentle death,
> Waiting to hush our latest breath,
> O praise him, alleluia,
> Thou leadest home the child of God,
> And Christ our Lord the way has trod;
> O praise him, alleluia.[29]

Much of the suffering associated with overstrenuous efforts to hold back the inevitable would be avoided if only such attitudes were once again common. From a Christian perspective death is believed to be the gateway to a new, richer and fuller life with God. If such beliefs are true, then when death comes in the fullness of time it should be embraced and accepted.

8 Does choosing death imply despairing of God's goodness?

We have already seen that no prohibition of suicide can straightforwardly be derived from biblical teaching. It is however strongly associated with traditional assumptions about divine providence, the virtues of patience and suffering, and the sense that actually to kill oneself is ultimately to despair of the loving purposes of God. The presumption here is that an authentic

Christian attitude shows itself in accepting in patience what God has willed. The problem is that the framework of belief here presupposed is not one which the typical contemporary Christian, whether priest or lay, seriously believes today. As we have already seen, the Christian understanding of providence has profoundly changed in relation to disease. It is no longer seen as a divine visitation or judgement sent to punish our wickedness or try our patience. Instead, illness is viewed by Christians as well as secularists as something due to natural causes which science can investigate and may be able to cure or alleviate. And the same spirit of autonomy which leads us to combat disease while we can, may also lead us to call off the battle and surrender to death when that seems the inevitable outcome.

9 The implication of Christ's 'golden rule' for suicide and euthanasia

One key principle for a Christian ethic is the yardstick recommended by Jesus in what Christians regard as his 'golden rule' from the Sermon on the Mount, namely, 'Always treat others as you would like them to treat you.'[30] Throughout life, one's hope is that if one falls ill, one will be able to obtain medical help to be restored to life and vitality. On this principle one would seek to ensure that medical treatment was as widely available as possible to all persons suffering any kind of disease or infirmity, whether of mind or body. Doctors and nurses who minister to the sick in this way are widely recognized by Christians as genuine agents and embodiments of God's providential love. Christians often describe the professions of medicine and nursing as 'vocations', that is, jobs which people may feel called by God to undertake for the good of humanity. I suggest the same principle should be upheld when obedience to the golden rule leads a doctor to help a patient out of terminal and hopeless misery.

The key assumption being made here is that in all circumstances where one might judge it morally justified for people to end their lives it would be equally justifiable for others to help them. That seems to me the clear implication of the golden rule. Suicide is not always easy or practical for a hospitalized patient who may only be able to save up sleeping pills or analgesics for a mortal overdose by forgoing their use in the previous days at the cost of hours of pain or wakefulness. Assisted suicide (i.e. euthanasia) is often very much the preferred option, and in circumstances where patient and doctor agree that this is the best course for that individual it seems right that it should not be prevented. Euthanasia has two further advantages over suicide. First is the fact that if the patient has to act alone, he or she may die prematurely at a time of temporary depression or pain, whereas if discussion with informed medical opinion is possible, the decision may be delayed until there really is no more likelihood of worthwhile life. Secondly, under the present law, suicide must almost always be a solitary and furtive death, for if relatives or friends were present at the time of the act they could be prosecuted as accomplices. However, if euthanasia were to become permissible, a patient could die with family and friends around the bedside.

It is also important for society as a whole that knowledge about, and access to, easy means of killing oneself should continue to be relatively restricted. Suicide is often a temptation to teenagers who are in a temporary state of depression but actually have good grounds for confidence in their futures. In such cases their ignorance of easy means of self-destruction often serves as a useful deterrent, and it is good that this should continue.

10 Is a request for euthanasia a denial of Christian hope?

Some suggest that to accept that one is not going to recover, and therefore to request help to die, is an act of faithless despair, a proclamation of hopelessness, and as such an offence against two of the central theological virtues – faith and hope. Here it is important that we confine ourselves to the very limited context of our discussion. We are considering cases where there are no realistic grounds for supposing that recovery is possible, and where even if some limited remission might occur, it would at best be temporary. There seems no virtue, whether theological or other, in self-delusion. Honest appraisal and a willingness to face reality seem far more appropriate stances. Moreover, it would be a total denial of the most basic Christian beliefs to limit hope to this world. As St Paul puts it, 'If it is for this life only that Christ has given us hope, we of all people are most to be pitied.'[31] And if one is speaking of hope in the context of the three theological virtues of faith, hope and love, it is worth reminding ourselves that, from a New Testament perspective, faith and love 'both spring from that hope stored up for you in heaven.'[32] When one speaks of the 'Christian hope' one is speaking of the historic Christian belief in a life after death. This is the context in which faith and hope are being considered. In a situation where a person's life is clearly drawing to its close, it could be an affirmation of faith, hope and love for a person voluntarily to choose death, entrusting his or her destiny into the loving hands of God.

The understanding of God presupposed here is that picture of God which is most distinctive of Jesus, namely that God is like a loving father always ready to accept his prodigal children.[33] Clearly on some other understandings of God, suicide would be the ultimate folly. If God were like a heavenly tyrant who would damn a suicide to endless punishment on the analogy of a ruler who might sentence to death a deserter in time of war, then euthanasia would be an act of unimaginable folly. But this view of God is really incompatible with the picture given to us in the teaching of Jesus, and though accepted by some in the past has little support in contemporary Christianity. New Testament criticism has shown fairly conclusively that the analogy of fatherhood was very rare in ancient Judaism prior to Jesus, and yet was Jesus' own constant usage concerning God. It is also apparent that Jesus' teaching of the necessity for forgiveness was the most controversial aspect of his thought, and is therefore almost certainly distinctive of him. Given this, a Christian may feel confident that God would show the same love and care to an actual suicide as Jesus' modern followers in the Samaritan movement seek to show to those who only make the attempt.

11 Is a suicide like a deserter or an uninvited guest?

The comparison of a suicide with a deserter abandoning his post while under attack seems most inept in the kind of euthanasia we are discussing. Given belief in any kind of providential order, one might conclude that the onslaught of terminal illness was the clearest possible indication of a divine intention to recall one to another station. Hence the grounds for condemning suicide in Blackstone's *Laws of England* as an 'invasion' of the Almighty's prerogatives by 'rushing into his presence uncalled for'[34] simply do not apply in the cases we are considering. Indeed, one might even regard a person requesting euthanasia in the context of terminal illness as showing commendable zeal in promptly responding to a divine summons rather than seeking every conceivable means to delay such a response! As David Hume put it in his classic essay, 'whenever pain and sorrow so far overcome my patience, as to make me tired of life, I may conclude that I am recalled from my station in the clearest and most express terms.'[35] In the Bible, Job reached the same conclusion, and in speech after speech describes the symptoms of his various illnesses as the harbingers of the death he longs for: 'Death would be better than these sufferings of mine. I have no desire to live.'[36]

12   Is it good for us to suffer?

One traditional Christian objection to euthanasia is that suffering is part of life, given by God to school our character and test our fortitude. To opt out of suffering is a repudiation of the opportunities that suffering provides for spiritual growth. What a dying Christian should do is rather to unite his or her sufferings with the sufferings of Christ, and to offer them up to God. On this view the pain and deprivation of terminal illness are something to be stoically accepted as part of the total experience of life which must be endured and not run away from. The argument is open to two serious objections. The first is that the theory does not correspond with human experience, since there is a great deal of evidence to show that suffering, however bravely borne, is rarely ennobling. The second is that the theory ought not to be used as an argument against euthanasia unless one is prepared to accept other implications of the hypothesis and refrain from administering analgesics. Yet virtually no one today takes that line. Almost everyone concerned with the dying accepts the duty and responsibility to do everything in one's power to minimize the discomfort of the terminally ill. The goal of palliative medicine is to search for a balance of medication at precisely the right dosage to control all pain. If suffering were genuinely believed to be good, this would not be the policy that was followed.

13 Euthanasia as a letting-go of life

One important argument for euthanasia is that it is a natural extension of the success of modern medicine. It is precisely because modern medicine has made it possible for us to choose to resist death that it should also be allowed to help us to choose when to abandon that resistance. Much of what I advocate would be gained by a greater spirit of 'letting-go' when there is no realistic hope of recovery. But this is not true of all cases.

On some occasions when it becomes apparent that further resistance to the illness is futile, the medical measures previously taken to combat the disease may make the process of dying significantly prolonged. Transplantation might be one example of such a measure, and the placing of people on life-support systems to assist breathing or to provide intravenous sustenance might be other examples. Having already massively intervened in the natural process, it seems wrong to let an arbitrary distinction between killing and letting-die prevent the patient being given the help needed.

14 Can euthanasia be reconciled with our duty to protect the vulnerable?

One argument against the view set forth here is that any legislation to permit euthanasia on request would put psychological pressure on aged and infirm people to ask for it even though it was not their real wish. A Christian should support the view that the law should protect vulnerable and dependent members of society from being exposed to such pressure when they are at their most vulnerable. I accept that this argument draws attention to a real problem. No matter how carefully permissive legislation is drawn it could be abused in the way feared. But what this objection fails to take note of is that this pressure would work in both directions. If euthanasia were legalized, many aged people who actually wanted to die would be put under enormous psychological pressure from relatives and friends not to ask for euthanasia but patiently to endure their sufferings. At present of course the position is even worse for those of the terminally ill who want euthanasia. They are not merely under pressure not to choose it. They simply have no choice.

15 The primacy of free choice

One much used argument for euthanasia is the importance of individual freedom and autonomy to live and die in the ways that are most conducive to our well-being as persons. What is needed is to try to create a society where people are free to be, as far as possible, responsible for their own lives, and free to make their own decisions as to what treatment or help they wish to have, including the right to choose between adequate hospice care in the terminal stages of illness or the equal right to seek for medical help to help in moving on to what Christians hope will be the fuller life of the world to come.

16 The opportunity euthanasia offers for a prayerful death

Historically it used to be the practice of all believers to summon a priest when death was thought near, so that the patient could die surrounded by an atmosphere of prayer and worship, and in the presence of family and friends. Modern technology has largely taken away that option. Many of us will die alone in a hospital bed, so attached to intravenous drips and other support systems that the older deathbed scene ceases to be possible. Yet if one were allowed and assisted to face the reality of the inevitable it would be possible for death to become an affirmation. One could imagine a situation where a Christian could say goodbye to family and friends, a Holy Communion service could be celebrated at the believer's bedside, and he or she could be given the last rites in preparation for the journey through death to the life immortal. In a context of faith this would seem a more Christian way of death than simply extending the time of our dying.

Notes

An earlier version of this chapter was published as 'Should Christians accept the validity of voluntary euthanasia?', in *Studies in Christian Ethics* for August/September 1995 and appears with permission.
1 House of Lords, *Report of the Select Committee on Medical Ethics* (London, HMSO, 1994).
2 Pope John Paul II, *Catechism of the Catholic Church* (London,

Chapman 1994, 491.
3 *Select Committee on Medical Ethics*, 24.
4 *Select Committee on Medical Ethics*, 48.
5 The giving of medicine is expressly forbidden in the early Christian book of teaching called the *Didache*, 2:2. It may also be forbidden in the Bible, in Galatians 5:20, where *pharmakeia* is banned. This is frequently translated as a ban on sorcery, but reference to any Greek dictionary will show that the word's primary meaning was the use of any drugs, potions or spells. This emphasis is even clearer in the use of the root word *pharmakon* (see for example Liddell and Scotts's *Greek–English Lexicon* of 1892).
6 For details see A. D. White, *A History of the Warfare of Science with Theology* (Cambridge, Mass., Harvard University Press, 1955), II, 36ff.
7 Derek Holmes, *The Triumph of the Holy See* (London, Burns and Oates, 1978), 82.
8 Cf. White, *Warfare of Science with Theology*, II, 36ff.
9 Genesis 3:16.
10 White, *Warfare of Science with Theology*, II, 63.
11 White, *Warfare of Science with Theology*, II, ch. 13.
12 St Thomas Aquinas, *Summa Theologiae*, Question 64, Article 5.
13 As Editor of *Ethics on the Frontiers of Human Existence* (New York, Paragon, 1992), and co-editor of *Perspectives on Death and Dying* (Philadelphia, Penns., The Charles Press, 1989).
14 *Hamlet*, I.ii.129ff; III.i.56ff.
15 Judges 17:28–30.
16 1 Samuel 31:3–6, 2 Samuel 1:11–27.
17 1 Maccabees 6:44.
18 2 Maccabees 14:41–2.
19 Matthew 27:5.
20 Matthew 26:24.
21 John 10:18.
22 John 10:10–16.
23 John 15:13.
24 Acts 20:16–38.
25 2 Timothy 4:6–8.
26 St Athanasius, *On the Incarnation*, ch.30 (London, Mowbray, 1963) 60–1.
27 Ecclesiasticus 41:1.
28 Ecclesiasticus 41:2.
29 *Hymns Ancient and Modern* (London, William Clowes, 1950), Hymn 172, verse 6.
30 Matthew 7:12.

31 1 Corinthians 15:9.
32 Colossians 1:5.
33 Luke 15:11–32.
34 W. Blackstone, *Commentaries on the Laws of England*, ed. A. Ryland (London, Sweet, Pheney, Maxwell, Stevens and Sons, 1829), IV, 169ff.
35 David Hume, 'On Suicide', in R. Wollheim, *Hume on Religion* (London, Fontana, 1963), 259.
36 Job 7:15; cf. 3:20–1, 7:3–7, 9:21, 10:1.

8

The case against euthanasia

STEPHEN WILLIAMS

1 Introduction

In presenting the case against euthanasia, there are two initial
questions that must be posed and answered. The first is: on what
basis is the case made out? Debate over euthanasia obviously
involves deep and interlocking moral convictions, but in what
looks like a society of moral strangers, the whole business of
persuasion is daunting unless we limit the constituency we are
hoping to persuade. At the same time, we are faced with questions of public policy which make such a limitation undesirable.
If we tried in this essay to develop a logic of moral reasoning and
persuasion on public issues in a pluralistic society, we would
never get on to the question of euthanasia itself. So one must be
content at this point simply to declare one's hand. I write as one
who is a Christian by conviction and a theologian by profession.
But this does not mean that what follows is simply a 'Christian'
or a 'theological' perspective *simpliciter*. For one thing, moral
reasoning involves attending to the conceptual dimensions of
issues in a way that is not specifically theological or religious. For
another, Christianity has been aptly described as aspiring to
'true humanism'.[1] It enshrines a vision of human flourishing
which may either have something in common with other, non-
Christian visions, or enable discussion with alternative
perspectives on common ground – at least in principle and at
least to some extent. I shall try to be faithful both to the public
context of the euthanasia debate and the convictions I bring to
it.

The second question gets our discussion proper off the
ground. How is euthanasia to be defined? Questions of definition

are capable of leading well-intentioned discussion into a swamp from which substantial conclusions will emerge only slowly and tentatively. Yet some definitional control is extremely important in the case of contemporary discussion of euthanasia. In one of the best brief statements of the case against euthanasia, Dr Henk Jochemsen outlined what euthanasia is not.[2] It does not apply in the following three cases. Firstly, there are cases when treatment which is medically useless is either not initiated or terminated ('uselessness' includes disproportion to possible benefit). Secondly, there are cases where treatment is designed to alleviate pain although it has the consequence of truncating life. Thirdly, there are cases where the patient refuses consent to medical treatment. Of course, these definitional limitations are controversial. From the definitional point of view, the first introduces the question of 'passive', the second of 'indirect', euthanasia. Definitions apart, knotty enough issues surface, for instance on the propriety of a distinction between intention and foresight. In taking Jochemsen's part here, we are not pre-empting the outcome of those discussions. But as a working definition of euthanasia we shall adopt either of the following definitions: 'the deliberate bringing about of the death of a human being as part of the medical care being given to him or her' 'or 'the death of a human being . . . brought about on purpose as part of the medical care being given to him [sic]'.[3] Contemporary advocates of voluntary euthanasia will find that definition acceptable so long as they are free to argue that if 'passive' or 'indirect' euthanasia is permitted one cannot consistently oppose active voluntary euthanasia. Although I do not think that the argument works, the case I shall make does not depend on that judgement. The above definitions have the advantage of setting discussion of euthanasia in the context of medical practice, which is the context of its public discussion.

In his essay on 'Euthanasia: a Christian view', Professor R. M. Hare argued that it was impossible on Christian premises to rule out euthanasia absolutely.[4] He took as fundamental in Christian ethics the golden rule that we do to others what we would have them do to us, which he proceeded to interpret and to apply to the discussion of euthanasia.[5] He offered the famous and historically realistic example of a driver slowly burning to death while trapped in his vehicle, pleading for a bystander to put him out of his misery. Hare concludes: 'Whatever principle we adopt about euthanasia, it is not going to be, if we consider this example seriously and apply Christ's words to it, the principle that euthanasia is always and absolutely wrong.'[6] But Hare seems to assume that the death of the lorry driver is a case of euthanasia or at least indistinguishable from it in any significant way.[7] However, one may agree that 'mercy killing' is in Hare's instance justified, and that its justification is relevant to the discussion of euthanasia without concluding that this warrants euthanasia as part of medical practice. But however we proceed on matters of definition, it is crucial that we keep in mind the medical context as we try to sustain a case against euthanasia. This case must begin with remarks on two themes important in the argument for euthanasia: autonomy and compassion. Accordingly, we turn to these.

2   Autonomy

The demand for autonomy, understood roughly as the right and power of self-determination, cannot be engaged with maximal effectiveness at the level of sheer argument. It is somehow lodged in 'modern' consciousness as an irreversible aspiration, at least for a significant number of people.[8] But arguments are certainly offered for giving autonomy its crucial due. One of these provides a useful *entrée* at this juncture. It comes from the pen of Tristram Engelhardt in a volume that has been described as 'what may be the fundamental work in bioethics for our time'.[9] Here, Engelhardt argued that since neither religion nor reason delivers universally acceptable moral norms, morality must be a matter of consent.

> Consent is cardinal because it is a source of authority. The appeal to consent requires neither an appeal to God nor a convincing rational argument about the best course of action. The treatment chosen for a patient is not *the* authorized treatment because it is the best form of treatment but because it is the treatment chosen by the patient and the physician.[10]

Although there are many examples, the issue of surrogate motherhood is especially prominent in his discussion. What makes contracts for surrogacy moral is that all involved give their consent. The argument obviously applies to euthanasia as well. It is a form of appeal to autonomy. Engelhardt's argument derives its force from the fact that he does not pretend to offer a desirable conclusion. Rather, he proposes it as inevitable. There is simply no other way of proceeding. However, as his case stands, this will not do. In contracts for surrogacy (as in cases of abortion, for example), all involved do *not* consent. The embryo or foetus has no say in the matter. Engelhardt can scarcely argue successfully that the foetus has no relevant rights on the ground that it cannot either give or withhold consent. For he would then be committed, for example, to the belief that infants have no right not to be tortured. If, out of moral conviction, I insist on the rights of a foetus not to be involved in surrogacy arrangements and Engelhardt insists that the foetus has no such rights, the sheer consent of the contracting parties in a surrogacy arrangement cannot establish the morality of the action. Consent in such a case may just be a privileged power and not a moral source. Why should we accord to it moral authority?

Now it may seem that in following the red herring of surrogacy we have got caught in a fatal current that will take us in the opposite direction of what was intended. For voluntary euthanasia is precisely about consenting parties and, on the legal plane, about the apposite contractual arrangement. The criticism made with regard to surrogacy fails in the case of euthanasia precisely for that reason. Of course, the cases are different, but the weakness in Engelhardt's argument alerts us to something fundamental about our approach to euthanasia, which is why it was introduced. Since the morality of surrogacy arrangements cannot be established in the way Engelhardt does, we are headed willy-nilly in the direction of public, direct, substantive discussion of ethical issues – just as Engelhardt tries to force us willy-nilly away from it – however hopeless it may seem, given our lack of religious or rational consensus. Engelhardt's argument just advertises the fact that social philosophy cannot be framed as though society were composed of consenting adults. It is largely composed of those not in a position to consent. It is when moral or ethical decisions must be taken on their behalf (as happens just as often when we take them on our own behalf) that we see the social inescapability of moral positions *not* based on consent. The ethical or the moral issue *per se* forces itself on us.[11]

Now one might rejoin that public policy should embody ethical positions on matters like surrogacy only when we are *forced* to such things. That is, when there are consenting parties, we need not offer any justification outside consent; wider justification is required only when we have no option. But this exhibits a highly dubious attitude to ethical issues which may ultimately turn out to be perverse. It is as though we are saying that although we are forced to moral justification in some instances, in other instances, involving fundamental questions of life, death and medical practice, we find no obligation to offer moral justification, consent being sufficient. Autonomy dislodges morality.

However, let us be clear on the point of these remarks. Of course, those who argue for voluntary euthanasia do not appeal solely to the autonomous right of self-determination in the context of a contractual agreement between patient and doctor freely undertaken. More substantial arguments are used. Yet the more weight we put on sheer autonomy, even if we adopt a different line from Engelhardt, the more a counterposition must press for a justification of the weight we do put. Why should the principle of autonomy carry more social weight than some principle like, for instance, sanctity of life? Is autonomy some kind of universal ethical principle? Is there an intuition to the effect that 'formal' qualities of an action (that it is autonomous) deserve social protection more than 'material' moral convictions (e.g. about the sanctity of life)? Whence and why the centrality of autonomy? The sheer fact that society is composed as it is, with its vast number of powerless dependants, should alert us to the possibility that 'autonomy' enjoys far too much unchallenged primacy in our ways of thinking.

3 Compassion

The weight of the argument for euthanasia can be variously distributed. The demands of compassion are often to the forefront, especially at popular level. All parties to the debate agree that the law constrains our autonomy in some respects, but some maintain that if it stands in the way of voluntary euthanasia, it consigns to illegality compassionate action. The counterargument, invested with the weight of centuries of tradition and medical practice, is that compassionate action must be lodged within an order where it is morally acknowledged that life is sacred. In terms of the historic evolution of ideas, this is where the clash of views is keenest and most dramatic. Those who advocate euthanasia claim that a sanctity-of-life principle thwarts compassion by its absolutism, bestowing on biological life some worth intrinsically greater than what can be measured in terms of quality, not to mention crushing the demand for autonomy. What are we to make of this? One point must be granted right away.

Those who oppose euthanasia on the grounds of sanctity of life often appear to be sponsoring a cold, inflexible absolutism, a rule of law in the form of a moral principle that has priority over the personal and the particular. It can appear bloodless and compassionless. The question is whether this is true to the principle and whether this appearance is rightly remedied by challenging the principle. Let us be clear that mainstream medical practice has always operated in accordance with particular cases and judged in accordance with their diverse peculiarities on questions of efficacy and point of treatment, projected quality of life and so forth. Sanctity of life has never meant dodging demanding judgements on what constitutes extraordinary or artificial treatment. Emphatically it has not meant the sheer protraction of biological life as the overriding goal of medicine or the proper expression of the principle. Intellectual and moral perplexities are unavoidable. Nor can one skirt issues arising out of neo-cortical 'death', the persistent vegetative state, including whether or not there are distinctions between the moral bases of medical and nutritive treatment and the concomitant question of whether tube-feeding is the one or the other and of whether it matters. The principle of the sanctity of life does not universally dictate an unambiguous resolution to quandaries in medical ethics. But it does entail limits on the nature of morally permissible action in the taking of life such that it cannot be taken simply on the grounds that the patient is suffering and wants it taken. Compassion is ordered to the alleviation of suffering but not to the taking of life.

Note that ever since we touched on definition, our approach to euthanasia is implicitly in terms of taking the life of another. We should make this explicit. It is generally a mistake to subsume discussion of euthanasia under the discussion of suicide. Suicide is death by one's own hand. Although there is reference to 'assisted suicide' in the euthanasia debate, and although that is the proper way to refer to certain actions that have come up for discussion in that debate, the plea for euthanasia is basically the plea that we give legal sanction to the medical profession to take the life of patients under certain specified conditions. That is not to say that discussion of suicide is always and altogether irrelevant, which is why I referred to 'general' mistakenness. It can present moral issues highly relevant to the question of euthanasia. But euthanasia is not a case of suicide.[12]

There are at least three dangers in cutting off compassion from a limiting substantive principle of the sanctity of life.

(1) It becomes difficult to ward off the demand for non-voluntary euthanasia. At present, the public argument is over voluntary, not non-voluntary, euthanasia. Suppose, however, that compassion is not borne along by a relevant principle of the sanctity of life, so that life is measured by its perceived quality and quality becomes a measure of the value of human life. If compassionate action in such cases allows euthanasia for those who request it, why should it not for those who do not? It is true that infants and the gravely mentally retarded cannot consent to euthanasia. Yet why should this be to their disadvantage? Why should their inability to express preference shut them off from the right to be subjects of compassionate non-voluntary euthanasia? Is it compassionate to deny them any such right?[13]

(2) It revolutionizes the philosophy and practice of medicine with deleterious effects. The doctor becomes professionally neutral in the matter of life and death. Her or his skills are directed to the clinical relief of suffering but no longer regulated by principles intrinsic to the profession, according to which patient and doctor operate within a broader moral framework instead of a narrower consensual framework. As a result, another route to non-voluntary euthanasia is opened. Because euthanasia is no longer professionally alien to medical practice, the elderly or chronically ill may begin to fear that relatives or friends will persuade doctors to perform euthanasia. Neither professional practice nor personal compassion are grounded in a sufficient principle of the sanctity of life that reassures the disadvantaged that they have nothing to fear. If one wants evidence that their fears are fully justified, the experience of the Netherlands is telling.[14]

(3) Compassion itself, considered under its emotional aspect, may dry up. In his preface to *The Genealogy of Morals*, written in 1887, Nietzsche wrote: 'I began to understand that the constantly spreading ethics of pity, which had tainted and debilitated even the philosophers, was the most sinister symptom of our sinister European civilization . . .'[15] He was reacting against Schopenhauer *inter alios*. Schopenhauer offered a relevant statement of his own position in the essay *On the Basis of Morality*, in which he traced moral action back to a fundamental sympathy, a deep compassion, which unites us with our fellow humans in distress.[16] As firmly as he rejected a basis for morality in divine command, he rejected it in what he took to be its secular counterpart, Kant's rational legislative will. Nietzsche's philosophy alerts us to at least two difficulties in Schopenhauer's argument. The first is that if compassion dries up, there is no basis for morality. The second is that Schopenhauer gives us no reason for believing that it cannot dry up.[17]

Nietzsche himself looked forward to a society where one had complete moral liberty to exercise or to withhold mercy, where one was not subject to compassionate feeling induced against one's will by the suffering of another. It is arguable that he was consistent in embracing such a prospect if morality is a purely creative enterprise. So morality tends to be, if we give pride of place to autonomy. '. . . The terms *autonomous* and *moral* are mutually exclusive . . .'[18] In contemporary post-Christian society, one fears that Nietzsche has put his finger on it. But with our reference to autonomy, we have come full circle. And with our reference to Christianity we arrive at the matter of specifically religious or theological principles.

4 In Christian perspective

Nothing in the argument so far amounts to anything like a conclusive case against euthanasia. It may appear that at most we have indicated its perils, but its perilous possibilities do not rule out the morality of an action, particularly if alternatives are themselves judged perilous or otherwise unsatisfactory. The fact is that, even if in our moral arguments we dwell on consequences, because there is no consensus on principles, we do not necessarily get very far. Consequences can be variously gauged, and disagreement can still exist on whether or not certain consequences are desirable. Of course, as far as this goes, the case for euthanasia is in no better shape than the case against. I have just sought to indicate the particular difficulties with which it is confronted, adducing reasons both for challenging the primacy of autonomy and for warning against the severance of compassion from a relevant principle of the sanctity of life. In Christian or wider theistic perspective, autonomy does not have the exalted status it often possesses in secular thought. It is questionable if it has logically any place at all within a theistic view of life, as Christian and atheist might alike maintain.[19]

Christianity does, however, speak of freedom. The dignity of freedom does not lie in freedom *per se* but in the use to which it can be put. Freedom is valuable because it can be instrumental in goodness. It may be that humans both have some knowledge of good and evil and have some freedom to do good or evil, but both the knowledge, such as it is, and the freedom, such as it is, signify something lacking, and not just something distinguishing, about human being. They presuppose the hiatus between the conditions of human existence and the supreme dignity of human being, which is to know God and to do good as the consuming purpose of human life. As Bonhoeffer argued with great force, in Christian perspective, humans are designed to know and to enjoy God and goodness and each other in that light; the knowledge of good and evil, and the capacity for good as well as evil, is a sign of human tragedy more than human dignity.[20] It may belong to human existence to possess a measure of freedom in order to realize that knowledge and exert that capacity. But God and the good can also be rejected, and one does not celebrate the capacity to do that.

In Christian, as in wider theistic, perspective, discussion of human flourishing, freedom or morality is stymied unless reference is made to the purpose of human life before God. The logic of Christian belief can scarcely lead elsewhere. Certainly, talk of purpose can be all too glib and suspiciously removed from human realities when invoked in the context of suffering and euthanasia. At the same time, to eliminate talk of it is impossible. Christians are pledged to bear witness to the transcendent reality of God as creator and redeemer of human life; to the intrinsic worth of human being precisely because it is generically constituted in the image of God; to the reality of a relationship with God which individuates each one generically in the divine image; to the responsibility to love one's neighbour as oneself even to the point where the consequences of what I do, as far as my neighbour is concerned, matters more than the comfort of what I do, as far as I am concerned.[21] This puts its peculiar complexion upon the question of euthanasia. The right to take one's own or another's life in scripture and according to Christian tradition is strictly demarcated precisely as a sign of the transcendent value of human life. It has usually been demarcation rather than absolute prohibition: the medieval virgin who took her own life rather than succumb to violation, or the magistrate who ordered a defensive and just war, figure in the tradition of permissible taking of life. But a broader right either to suicide or to murder cannot be derived from this and neither can permission for euthanasia as part of medical practice in the twentieth century.

To speak of transcendent divine purpose is certainly not to affirm that pain, suffering and indignity are purposeful in the sense that they are always to run their course in the name of the divine will. The fact that the greatest single contributor to the New Testament literature (Luke) was a physician sends an important signal in that respect.[22] But that people as they are – chronically ill, depressed, lonely, undignified, mentally incapable, deformed, in pain – that these are loved as they are, just because they are, by a God that they are humanly designed to know and to love – this cannot be affirmed by euthanasia. It can by strenuous action to relieve pain and the care developed in the tradition of hospices.[23]

> Why is light given to those in misery, and life to the bitter of soul, to those who long for death that does not come, who search for it more than for hidden treasure, who are filled with gladness and rejoice when they reach the grave? Why is life given to a man whose way is hidden, whom God has hedged in?

These are the words of Job, found in the canonical text of Jews and Christians (3:20–3). In the story, the Lord God scarcely rebukes or chastises Job for sentiments shared by many who request euthanasia. His religious comforters are the ones who receive the stick. But God does press Job towards a realization and a confession. If there is God and if God is creator, the search for purely immanent purposes in human life, the attempt to gauge its significance by its temporal course, in sickness and in health, is already a mistake. The response of faith offered by Paul in his letter to the Romans was: 'For none of us lives to himself alone and none of us dies to himself alone. If we live, we live to the Lord; and if we die, we die to the Lord. So, whether we live or die, we belong to the Lord' (14:7–8).

Secular advocates of euthanasia are right to draw our attention to the humanitarian summons to alleviate suffering. Religious advocates of euthanasia are right to draw our attention to the fact that death precedes the fulfilment of hope rather than proving its final destruction. But in a society where the humanitarian is not guaranteed to survive, and in a theology where the global consequences of action help to determine the nature of human decision before God, we should not entertain euthanasia. Nor is this because of possible, passing, uncertain, changing temporal or social circumstance. It is because humans are not the 'unlimited proprietors of their own persons'.[24] If they essay a unilateral declaration of independence they risk propelling society towards a consequential contempt for life.[25] We had better not discover what raw humanity is made of.[26]

Notes

[1]   A phrase popularized by the French philosopher, Jacques Maritain, *True Humanism* (London, Bles, 1938).

[2]   H. Jochemsen, 'A Christian evaluation of, and alternative to, euthanasia', available via the Prof. dr. G. A. Lindeboom Institute, Ede, Netherlands.

[3]   The first formulation is that of David Atkinson, *Pastoral Ethics in Medical Practice* (Tunbridge Wells, Monarch, 1989), 221; the second is from *Euthanasia and Clinical Practice* (London, Linacre Centre, 1982), 2.

[4]   In his *Essays on Religion and Education* (Oxford, Clarendon, 1992). His essay on 'Medical ethics: can the moral philosopher help?' gives a good indication of his method, in R. M. Hare, *Essays on Bioethics* (Oxford, Clarendon, 1993).

[5]   On the prescriptions of the golden rule, Hare remarks: 'I can think of no moral question on which they have a more direct bearing than

the question of euthanasia . . .' (op. cit., 72).

6   Op. cit., 75.

7   A close reading of the significant 'Anglican contribution to the debate on euthanasia', titled *On Dying Well* (London, Church House, 1975), will reveal the vacillation between thinking of the burning-lorry situation as one of euthanasia or one that helps to determine our views of euthanasia.

8   Don Cupitt, *Taking Leave of God* (London, SCM, 1980), ch.1.

9   I take this commendation of Marx Wartofsky from the cover of T. Engelhardt, *Bioethics and Secular Humanism: The Search for a Common Morality* (London, SCM/Philadelphia, Trinity, 1991).

10 Op. cit., 126ff.

11 I am assuming a typical modern democratic context where neither mere appeals to tradition nor totalitarian resolutions are judged acceptable.

12 An important religious angle on suicide is captured by the words of Madame de Staël: 'Though there be many crimes of a deeper dye than suicide, there is no other by which men appear so formally to renounce the protection of God', quoted by W. E. H. Lecky, *A History of European Morals* (London, 1869), vol. ii, p.47. In light of our later reference to Bonhoeffer, we note the summary but quite powerful discussion of suicide and the taking of life in *Ethics* (New York, Macmillan, 1965), p.155–73.

13 We should have to explore here the connections between arguments for euthanasia and abortion. For a statement of the fact that identity of 'ideological background' makes easy the slide from voluntary to non-voluntary (he calls it 'involuntary') euthanasia, see Jochemsen, op. cit., especially pp.5–7).

14 See John Keown, 'The law and practice of euthanasia in the Netherlands', *Ethics and Medicine*, 8, 3 (1992), 34–48.

15 *On the Genealogy of Morals* (New York, Vintage, 1969). Nietzsche's reference to Buddhism in particular can be generalized.

16 *On the Basis of Morality* (New York, Bobbs-Merrill, 1965).

17 I have sought to discuss Nietzsche and some further objections that might be made to connecting compassion with a sanctity-of-life principle in 'Bioethics in the shadow of Nietzsche', in N. de Cameron, J. Kilner and D. Scheidermeyer (eds.), *Bioethics and the Future of Medicine* (Carlisle, Paternoster, 1995).

18 Nietzsche, op. cit., 2.11.

19 The question whether theism logically affords space for autonomy can divide participants across and not along the theist–atheist divide. Some relevant probing takes place in John Macken's work, *The Autonomy Theme in the 'Church Dogmatics': Karl Barth and his Critics*

(Cambridge, CUP, 1990).

20 Op. cit., part 1.

21 Discussion of the social consequences of suicide are relevant here. It has been regarded as socially of deepest significance in terms of inducing guilt, grief and suicide-expectancy. Hume was very far off the mark when, in his defence of suicide, he said: 'A man, who retires from life, does no harm to society: he only ceases to do good; which, if it is an injury, is of the lowest kind . . .', 'Of suicide', in A. MacIntyre (ed.), *Hume's Ethical Writings* (New York, Macmillan, 1965). See the fallacious argument of the whole essay, which concludes that if human action to preserve life does not usurp divine prerogative, neither does human action to take it.

22 I assume the Lucan authorship of the Acts of the Apostles.

23 In this essay I am not giving its due importance to hospice work. The test of an authentic Christian moral stance is what is done about a situation and not just how it is morally regarded. Hospices are obviously not appropriate for all the cases where euthanasia is requested, but the underlying ethic of human life and dignity is apt.

24 The originator of this phrase is the deist Elihu Palmer: see Peter Gay, *Deism: An Anthology* (New York, Van Nostrand, 1968), 189.

25 Nietzsche explicitly arrives at this point in regard to physicians' attitudes to patients; see 'The twilight of the idols', in *The Twilight of the Idols/The Antichrist* (Harmondsworth, Penguin, 1990), 98ff. Nietzsche's conclusions are certainly repugnant to many in favour of euthanasia, and I am certainly not imputing Nietzschean attitudes to them. But before he is dismissed, the logic of the two preceding works, *Beyond Good and Evil* and *The Genealogy of Morals*, must be studied and successfully refuted.

26 It may be difficult to persuade that one is not scaremongering at this point. The Dutch situation needs scrutiny here. Ironically and sadly, Dutch physicians were admirably resistant to Nazi pressure for euthanasia. Whether or not invocation of the Nazis is scaremongering I cannot decide here, but see the celebrated essay on 'Medical science under dictatorship' by Dr Leo Alexander, often reprinted, e.g. in *Ethics and Medicine*, 3, 2 (1987), where it should be read alongside the preceding essay by Dr Everett Koop, 'Decisions at the end of life'.

Part II
The Quest for Meaning and Purpose in Death

9

The near-death experience

PETER AND ELIZABETH FENWICK

1 Introduction

Concern about our immortality is an almost universal human preoccupation. Most cultures have embraced the notion that there is something beyond death, beyond the blackness of the grave. Those of us who embrace the Western Judaeo-Christian culture absorb from an early age the ideas that virtue now has its own reward later, that the universe is essentially moral and that there are absolute human values.

Increasingly, science presents us with a picture of a much more mechanical universe in which there is no absolute morality and humans have no purpose and no personal responsibility except to their culture and biology. We no longer live in an age when faith is sufficient; we demand data, and we are driven by data. The near-death experience holds a fascination because it seems to provide just such data; data that illuminate our current ideas of life after death, including heaven and hell, and perhaps even offer a promissory note that there may be some foundation for human hopes of immortality.

There is nothing particularly new about the notion that one can die and live to tell the tale. Written descriptions of similar experiences abound in myths and legends going back well over 2,000 years. It is likely that for as long as human beings have been aware of the certainty of death they have contemplated the possibility of survival and have wondered what happens next. The most ancient burial sites contain artefacts that suggest belief in the survival of some aspect of the human being after bodily death. Plato (427–347 BC) at the end of the *Republic* tells the story of a soldier, Er, who was thought to have died on the field of battle. He revived on his funeral pyre and described a journey out of his body to a place of judgement, where souls were sent to heaven or to a place of punishment, according to the life they had lived on earth. Before reincarnation they were sent across a river, where their experience of heaven was wiped from their memory. However, Er himself was sent back to tell others what he had seen.

For the scientist, the near-death experience (NDE) is intriguing for many reasons. One is that it is very common, and another that research suggests it is cross-cultural. The results of one National Opinion Poll in America suggest that more than one million Americans have 'seen the light'. Could any experience that is so common not have some influence on the way we view life and death? Indeed, it might even be the very source of our ideas of an afterlife. Many believe that the NDE gives us glimpses of heaven (or hell). It is, however, just as reasonable to assume that it is the NDE itself that may have shaped our ideas about heaven and hell.

No two NDEs are identical. However, certain common features occur repeatedly. I will here briefly outline these:

(1) *Positive emotional feelings* Overwhelming feelings of peace, joy and bliss are the first and most memorable part of the NDE for many experiencers. Any feelings of pain that the earthly body may have been experiencing drop away.

(2) *Out-of-body experiences* These usually occur at the beginning of the experience. The person feels as though he or she is slowly rising out of the body, and can look down on it from some objective vantage point, while floating weightless above it.

(3) *The dark tunnel* The person may enter darkness, usually passing rapidly through a dark tunnel with no physical effort. Experiencers report seeing, at the end of the tunnel, a pinpoint of light that grows larger as it is approached. Some, on the other hand, describe a tunnel of light, not darkness.

(4) *The light* Experiencers nearly always describe the light at the end of the tunnel as white or golden; brilliant, but not dazzling. Often, it seems to act as a magnet, drawing the person towards it, and it has a quality of warmth.

(5) *The being of light* At some point the person may meet a

'being' of light. Some may describe this as an obviously religious figure such as Jesus. Others simply describe it as a 'presence' that they feel to be God or Godlike. This is nearly always an intensely emotional experience. Experiencers often say they cannot find words to describe their feelings.

(6) *The barrier* Sometimes the person senses a barrier between him- or herself and the light. It may be a physical barrier, i.e. a person, a gate or fence. At other times, it is simply a feeling that the person knows this is a point beyond which one cannot pass.

(7) *The landscape* Experiencers often say that they have visited another country, usually an idyllic pastoral scene, brilliantly coloured, filled with light, or that they have glimpsed such a place beyond the barrier.

(8) *Meeting friends and relatives* Occasionally experiencers meet other people, usually dead friends or relatives or, more rarely, people who are still alive and sometimes strangers.

(9) *The life review* At some point in the experience the person may see events from his life flash before him. A few experiencers say they have felt they are being weighed up, experiencing a sort of day of judgement in which their past actions are reviewed. Some experience a life preview; that is, events are unfolded to them that are to take place in the future, and sometimes they are told there are tasks ahead of them that they must go back to complete.

(10) *The point of decision* Often, although experiencers want to stay, they realize that it is 'not their time to go'. They may make the decision to go back themselves, usually because they realize that their families still need them. Sometimes the decision is made for them, and they are sent back either by the 'being of light', or by the friends or relatives they have met, often, too, with a sense that they have unfinished business to complete before they are finally allowed to 'cross the barrier'.

(11) *The return* Sometimes the person simply finds him- or herself back in his or her body. Sometimes the experiencer is aware of 'snapping back' into the body.

(12) *The aftermath* Experiencers usually vividly remember the NDE for years, often for a whole lifetime. Experiencers report that they returned changed in some way, often,

though not always, permanently. Subsequent loss of fear of death is common. Some believe that they have been given psychic powers such as precognition or the gift of healing, following the experience.

It is understandable that we should want to examine such experiences in detail and subject them to scientific scrutiny. It is also important to bear in mind that the assumptions which underpin our current science contain limitations which may prevent science from obtaining a meaningful explanation of such subjective experiences. Our current science is based on the concept of an independent external world which is common to each observer, and a consensus view allows us to set up and test hypotheses which can be verified between independent observers. What is becoming clear from neuroscience, however, is that the view we take of an independent external world is a psychological construct and contains only subjective experience. Although it is reasonable in most situations to consider this subjective world as objective, this view breaks down when one is considering only psychological experiences which appear to have no foundation in a common external reality. Thus the NDE sets a challenge to our scientific assumptions and to the explanations that we can put forward about our own subjective experiences.

Our current scientific model argues for no validity to subjective experience except that it is based in brain structure. Although this is a reasonable scientific view to take, it does mean that ultimately the only explanations we can give of the NDE must be descriptions of brain function. At the present time, neuroscience is progressing extremely fast. On the one hand, with molecular genetics the basic structures responsible for transmission between nerve cells are much better understood, and show a picture of enormous complexity. At a higher level of organization, the action of groups of cells in systems shows that a person's experience is not a unity but is composed of numerous independent functions, any one of which may be lost, and all of which have to be integrated in some way to give a transient view of the present moment. The initiation of action, what we could loosely term free will, has a centre within the brain, as do our feelings of guilt, our appreciation of music and the finer sensitivity of being able to understand other people's minds.

Thus neuroscience is arguing for a highly structured and localized brain with the possibility of a potential explanation for all we think of as the higher qualities of man. On the other hand, there is accumulating evidence that mind may be able to act directly on matter, that is, the mind is not confined within the skull. Results from the meta-analyses of the Ganzfeld experiments and from Bob John's experiments at Princeton provide powerful scientific evidence for an action of mind at a distance. These two trends, the increasing ability of neuroscience to explain mind on the one hand, and the increasing evidence that mind acts beyond the skull on the other, suggest that a new theory of mind is required. The form of this new theory is likely to follow that of the new physics in that mind is more likely to be seen as acting as a field rather than just as a simple distillation of neuronal firing patterns locked within a neuronal network.

2 Population surveyed

The remainder of this chapter will be a descriptive analysis of first-hand accounts from people who wrote to us or to David Lorimer (Chair of the International Association of Near Death Studies, UK). People wrote from all areas of England, though the greatest number was from the south-east. Fewer responses were forthcoming from Wales, fewer still from Scotland and only two from Ireland.

From more than 1,000 accounts, we selected 500 that represented prototypical NDEs. We excluded experiences that seemed due to dreams, fantasy or recreational drug use, as well as those that seemed to arise in a pathological setting in correspondents in psychological turmoil. We also excluded those in which disorders of brain function such as epilepsy were present, as well as those where the experience described was clearly directly dependent on brain pathology and therefore not in any sense related to being near death either physically or psychologically.

We did *not* exclude those prototypical NDEs that occurred when the person was technically not 'near death'. This allowed us to test hypotheses that suggest that there are differences between the experiences of those who were truly near death and those who were not.[1]

We sent the selected 500 respondents a questionnaire that we had devised. In constructing the questionnaire we took into account previous questionnaires.[2] However, we felt that the field of NDEs had progressed to a point where we needed to ask different questions. The questionnaire aimed to obtain, in a standardized format, as much detail as possible about the NDE, the individual who experienced it, and the effect that the experience had on the individual's life.

We received more than 360 replies. This analysis, however, comprises only the first 344. Of these, 78 per cent were women, 22 per cent men; 59 per cent married, 15 per cent divorced, and 10 per cent single; 80 per cent were eighteen years of age or over (adults) at the time of the experience; 9 per cent were ten or younger; 51 per cent described themselves as Church of England, 12 per cent Roman Catholic; 19 per cent as belonging to other Christian denominations, and 1 per cent Jewish; 8 per cent described themselves as agnostic, and 2 per cent as atheist. In population surveys, approximately 25 per cent of people will claim to be either atheist or agnostic. Therefore, the 10 per cent we found is surprisingly small. This finding could be related to the way we worded the question. It specified 'religion' and it is possible that some respondents may have answered giving the religion in which they were raised rather than their present belief. Fifty-six per cent said they 'did not go to worship' (were not churchgoers). However, 16 per cent said they went to church every week. Thirty-nine per cent said religion was important to them, 41 per cent that it wasn't, while 20 per cent replied that perhaps it was.

We specified nine categories of occupation. These categories are a variation of the Registrar General's classification. We were interested in occupation because other surveys had clearly indicated a relationship between education and frequency of NDEs. Twenty-nine per cent of the sample were professional or equivalent, 17 per cent skilled or semi-skilled, 25 per cent housewives or househusbands, and 23 per cent retired. Only 3 per cent were students and 2 per cent were unemployed.

As well as asking about the NDE itself, we tried, as far as possible, to discover the circumstances in which it occurred, and the state of consciousness of the person when the experience began. We asked: 'What was your state of consciousness at the outset of the experience?' One-third reported that they were awake, 13 per cent asleep; 14 per cent under anaesthesia, 17 per cent unconscious, 20 per cent semi-conscious, and 3 per cent said that they were confused.

Concerning the circumstances in which the experience occurred, 10 per cent reported that it occurred as the result of an accident, 9 per cent during heart attack, 15 per cent during childbirth. The largest group, 23 per cent, said it arose during illness. These illnesses varied widely, were usually severe but not always life-threatening. Another 21 per cent described the experience as occurring during an operation, and 20 per cent during 'other circumstances' not included above. In only 2 per cent did the experience arise during a suicide attempt. It is important to note that only 37 per cent were receiving drugs at the time of the experience, which means that nearly two-thirds were drug free.

We also wanted to know how many people knew about NDEs before their experience. This is important, because, if an experiencer had prior knowledge of NDE, it would be reasonable to suppose that this knowledge could to some extent influence the experience. We found that only a tiny proportion, 2 per cent, said they first became aware of NDEs before their own experience. The vast majority claimed to know nothing about the phenomena and only became aware much later when they happened on accounts of others' experiences.

Most, 79 per cent, had one NDE only, though a surprising number, 12 per cent, had two, and a few, 9 per cent, said they had three or more. Clearly the NDE does not confer lifelong immunity. Evidence suggests that there may even be an 'NDE-prone personality', or that one experience may, in some way, facilitate another.

Ring and Rosing have suggested that NDEs are most likely to occur in persons who had had a difficult birth and were, therefore, possibly mildly brain-damaged, or in those who had had a particularly unhappy childhood.[3] We tested these ideas and found, that in our sample these did not hold true. Only 27 per cent reported having had a difficult or prolonged birth, and only 17 per cent said their childhood had been unhappy; 82 per cent described their childhood as average or above average happiness.

Hellish NDEs are rare. Only three persons in our sample described their experiences as 'hellish'. Other investigators have found no hellish experiences.[4] A few have collected a few accounts of journeys to hell and back,[5] but overwhelmingly it seems that glimpses of heaven are easier to come by in the NDE than glimpses of hell. Is this because, where life after death is concerned, we are all pastmasters at giving ourselves the benefit of the doubt? A Gallup survey certainly found that most people, even if they believed in hell, rated their personal chance of ending up there as 'small'.

Sabom has suggested that the reason that so few hellish experiences have been described is that they are quickly forgotten.[6] Our own impression is that those who had these bad experiences were strongly affected by them, but much more reluctant to talk about them than people who had had positive experiences. 'I had a hell-type experience twenty years ago', said one woman, 'and it has haunted me ever since.' She refused to give any more details. When negative experiences do occur, they seem to be just as powerful and just as memorable as positive ones. However, it is also possible that a few people manage to suppress negative experiences and so simply do not remember them.

3   Content of the experiences

We were interested in the content of the experiences and extracted from the literature those features we felt were most important. In answer to the question, 'Did you experience any darkness?', 66 per cent or two-thirds had not experienced darkness. This is a surprising finding in view of the numbers of experiences which describe catastrophic brain dysfunction when unconsciousness and darkness would be almost guaranteed. This finding will certainly require further investigation in a later study. In answer to the question, 'Did you experience any light?', 72 per cent said they had. Just under half of the group, 49 per cent, experienced a 'tunnel'. One explanation of the tunnel and light phenomena maintains that random firing of the neurones in the visual cortex precipitated by cerebral anoxia leads to the impression of light. As this area expands, the impression of light increases, and thus the experiencer has the feeling that he or she is approaching the light, which subjectively gives the impression of a tunnel. We certainly found a relationship between the tunnel and the light.[7] Both light and tunnel were seen by 133 people; only twenty-eight people had a tunnel experience without light.

However, ninety-three people did see the light, but no tunnel (Chi 17.5<0).

Most near-death experiencers describe the colour of the light (usually but not always seen at the end of a tunnel) as being either brilliant white or golden. Few previous authors have given the frequency with which experiencers saw other colours. We asked, 'If you saw a light, what colour was it?' Of the sample, 56 per cent described it as brilliant white, 21 per cent as golden. Other colours described were red (2 per cent), orange (3 per cent), yellow (6 per cent), green (2 per cent), blue (3 per cent). Another 7 per cent described the light as having no colour, but did not associate this with white. Analysis of the data suggests that many people describe the light as having a quality of warmth, and it is perhaps significant that only 5 per cent of the respondents describe the colour of the light as being at the colder (blue) end of the spectrum.

We asked if they had experienced a landscape, and 76 per cent said they had. The descriptions suggest that the landscape is usually highly coloured and idealized, and resembles an English garden or pastoral scene in summer. Experiencers described no winter gardens, no dying plants, no moors or mountains. Paths led through the gardens of brightly coloured flowers. Some experiencers recognized and named the flowers and commented on the luxuriant blooms.

I was just in a wonderful peace and wellness in a beautiful landscape setting of grass, lawns and trees and brilliant light . . .

. . . a garden where surely beauty had found its name. This was an old-fashioned, typically English garden with a lush green velvet lawn, bounded by deep curving borders brimming with flowers, each flower nestling within its family group, each group proclaiming its presence with a riot of colour and fragrance as if blessed by a morning dew. The entrance to the garden was marked by a trellis of honeysuckle so laden that you had to crouch down to pass beneath while at the other end a rustic garden gate led to the outside. It was here that my walk through was to end as I was gently led through to the other side . . .

These gardens are unusual in their absence of wildlife. We were pleased to find that these visions of paradise contained no midges, snakes or spiders, but they were devoid of other animals as well. Only one respondent mentioned 'all the dogs of my life' bounding over the hill to greet him.

The next question, 'Did you experience any colours?', may have been difficult for the subjects to answer, because it is not specific. It is difficult to know to what our respondents were referring when they answered either yes or no, but this question immediately followed the question concerning the landscape, it is reasonable to assume that the answers also concerned the landscape. Only a third of the sample, said they had experienced colours. 'I was floating through swathes of wonderful, beautiful, translucent colours, more beautiful than any I had ever seen on earth.'

4 Music

We were interested in the frequency with which music is heard, as some previous reports mention the presence of heavenly choirs and heavenly music. Our research suggests music is relatively rare; only 19 per cent described hearing it. In the individual accounts, the music was usually described as 'wonderful'. It is worth noting that there is scientific evidence which shows that music is elaborated in the right temporal lobe. Damage to this area can result in the inability to understand musical sequences, so although the notes are still heard it is impossible to extract the melody. Rhythm is also located in this area of the brain. Thus, damage to this area will result in lack of musical appreciation. A recent finding suggests that concordant musical sounds are specifically picked up by the right hippocampus, a structure in the right temporal lobe. The left hippocampus detects discordant notes. It is thus possible to hypothesize that during the hearing of heavenly music, which to Western ears usually means concordant music, the right temporal lobe is activated.

5 Positive and negative emotions

Strong positive emotions are reported commonly in NDEs, and our questions were directed at trying to define more accurately the feelings described. We defined three dimensions: calmness and peace; joy; and love. Overall, 82 per cent felt calmness and peace, 40 per cent felt joy, and 38 per cent felt love. There was a clear overlap between categories, with most people feeling calmness and peace. Of those who felt joy and love, 9 per cent felt joy only, and 8 per cent felt love only, while 28 per cent felt both joy and love.

> . . . I experienced a feeling of utter peace and was conscious that I was smiling.

> . . . I felt a complete sensation of happiness and contentment.

> For that is the dominant feeling, the memory and knowledge of ultimate, total peace.

> I was convinced no living person could experience such joy. The only way I can explain it is, think of the happiest moment of your life, and when you do, that happiest moment is awful pain compared to what you feel . . .

> I was filled with elation and pure joy – the nearest description of the feeling was as a child on the last day of the summer term knowing six weeks holiday loomed ahead full of freedom and sunshine. I felt absolutely no fear at all, just utter pleasure as if I was off somewhere wonderful.

With the peace often comes a feeling of profound knowledge, a realization that one has been given the answer to all the secrets of the universe.

> . . . I was peaceful, totally content, and I understood I was born on earth and knew the answer to every mystery – I was not told, I just knew, the light held all the answers.

> All around me were the answers to everything, no puzzles because I had been given the key to understanding everything.

> Sadly, when this woman came back:
> I kept the sense of having had a wonderful experience, a revelation. Unfortunately the magic key to understanding, Pure Logic, had been taken from me. I still see through a glass darkly.

Because many of these experiences are catastrophic and overwhelming, we expected that a large proportion of our subjects would feel fear. In the near-death literature very few people report feeling fear, and usually the onset of the experience is heralded by peace and calmness. It was thus important to ask a specific question about fear which we predicted would be present. The results do not support this predicition, as only 15 per cent reported feeling any fear. We are also concerned about feelings of loss, either the loss of family and friends or the loss of life. Again, we predicted at some point in the experience a high rate of feelings of loss. Again the data do not support the prediction; only 9 per cent described these feelings. It may be that only those with positive experiences tended to write to us; or that those who had negative experiences tended to suppress them. It seems more probable that in the overwhelming majority of NDEs, the predominant emotion is positive, and that it is only in the absence of such positive emotion that any element of fear is experienced.

6 Meeting people

In the literature, it is usual for the near-death experiencer to meet a person during the experience. Usually, it is a friend or relative who has died; less often it is a stranger or a religious figure.

Only 38 per cent of our sample met someone they knew. Of these, half met only relatives, 9 per cent only friends, and 10 per cent met both, while 28 per cent met people they knew who were neither relatives nor friends. The NDE literature suggests that when relatives or friends are met, adults usually meet the dead whereas children meet living friends. In our study, however, 39 per cent of adults are little different from children in this respect, and secondly, the inclusion of living people in the scenario suggests that the psychological model is not entirely consistent with an after-death experience.

Because of a wide variation in the severity of the incident causing the NDE, it could be predicted that subjects who were not actually very near death would be more likely to see living than dead people. However, the answer to our question, 'Were you pronounced dead?' showed no significant difference between those who were and those who were not.

A number of people saw strangers. It would be logical to assume that one would be most likely to see people one knew, but more than 40 per cent said they were aware of strangers. It would also be expected that heaven would be populated by religious figures, but only one-third (34 per cent) admitted meeting a religious figure. Forty people who described their religion as important, and twenty-three for whom it was not important, saw religious figures. Sixty-one people whose religion was important, and seventy-nine for whom it was unimportant, did not see religious figures. The relationship between thinking religion important and the seeing of religious figures was highly significant (p = 0.006).

7 Memories

Investigation of memory has shown that different types of memory are processed in very specific brain areas. Memories dealing with words (verbal memory) are processed by the dominant (usually left) hippocampus, whereas spatial data are processed in the non-dominant (usually right) hippocampus. It is thus possible, by looking at the structure of the memories which are evoked, to decide whether or not they are recalled mainly from the left or the right hemisphere of the brain.

Although some researchers have found a high incidence of past-life reviews in the NDE,[8] in our sample, it was rare. Only 12 per cent said that scenes from the past came back to them; 9 per cent said that they experienced memories from their life. In only about half of these (53 per cent) were the memories considered significant. With regard to the part of the brain that was activated, 44 per cent of these said that the memories were mainly pictorial, 28 per cent that they were mainly verbal, while 29 per cent said both. There is thus a clear indication that memories were largely visio-spatial and coming mainly from the right hemisphere.

We also asked whether scenes from the future were seen in the experience. Only 13 per cent replied yes; 73 per cent said no. Of those who replied yes, 23 per cent said these were scenes of the world's future, 48 per cent that they were of their personal future; 29 per cent saw both. Later feelings of *déjà vu* are sometimes linked by the experiencer with these visions of the future. One person reported that it was as if he were remembering glimpses of a video he had once been shown.

8 Time and thinking

Both the process of thinking and the sense of time are said to be altered during NDEs. We tested this. In answer to the question, 'Did time seem to alter?', 64 per cent said it did. Of these, 12 per cent said that it went faster, 46 per cent that it slowed, and 41 per cent said that everything seemed to happen all at once.

Half the sample (49 per cent) felt that the speed of their thoughts was altered. Almost a third said they were incredibly fast (30 per cent); a third said they were faster than usual. Only a third said they were slower than usual.

9 The barrier

The barrier is a point in the experience beyond which the experiencer is unable to go; 24 per cent experienced a gate or border. Sometimes the barrier is simply a feeling that you can go no further, but often it takes a physical form:

> I was in a lane where there were very high ornamental golden gates, inside was the most beautiful garden . . . I pushed the gates and they gave way to my push, but try as I might I could not get in, there was something behind me on both sides which seemed to be stopping me from going in. I was so upset at not being able to get in, but in the end I gave up trying.

It is not entirely clear why there is a need for a barrier. It would be perfectly possible to go to heaven, have a day out playing in the wonderful and highly coloured countryside, and then as the light slowly sank in the west to be sent home back to your body. It does not work like that. It seems as if it is necessary for heaven to be divided into two parts, that which is accessible, and that which is not. There is marked psychological significance attached to this division. The implication is always that if you go beyond the barrier, then you will never return.

10 The return

Our entrance into heaven is involuntary. We are simply taken there by the experience. However, we are often allowed a hand in our return; 72 per cent said there was a decision to return. In 52 per cent of cases the patient made the decision personally; in 48 per cent it was made by someone else; 58 per cent wanted to return, 42 per cent did not. It seems that about half the people were sent back and half made a voluntary return. Asked whether they would like to have the experience again and continue, 52 per cent said they would, 48 per cent would not.

There is a significant relationship p<0 between not wanting to return and wanting the experience again. Of 134 who had wanted to come back, 55 wanted the experience again whereas 79 did not. Of the 89 who did not want to return, 64 wanted the experience again.

11 Transformation

Morse has suggested that the hallmark of the NDE is that it induces some change in the experiencer.[9] Asked whether they or their life had been changed by the experience, 72 per cent said that it had changed them in some way. By far the most common change reported was in people's attitudes towards death; 82 per cent said they now had less fear of death, though many still felt apprehensive about dying. This lack of fear of death is not necessarily linked to a conviction that there is an afterlife, and less than half (48 per cent) believed in personal survival after death. Often people feel that their experience is something they can use to reassure others about death.

> The experience has had a lasting effect upon my life: if that was 'near death' I have no fear when my time for dying comes. I look forward to it with expectation of that wonderful joy and peace.

> There may well be 'life after life' or it could be the way the brain shuts down, either way, death is something to look forward to, when it comes.

> When I awoke I felt very much at peace. I have since told people that I no longer fear death itself – I've never felt the need to talk about it but have happily related the events to any inquiring person . . .

> . . . when people tell me they are afraid to die I always come trotting out with this experience even if they do think I am nuts . . .

Any intense emotional experience, whether positive or negative, changes people in some way. The experience of the transforming light is for many the most profound emotional experience ever encountered. The feeling is one of being overwhelmed with universal love, of being accepted in totality by some loving being. The memory of this loving and complete acceptance seems to enable people to see themselves in a very different perspective, and in some way to feel and behave as a different person. There is a significant relationship (p<0.0008) between feelings of peace and calm during the experience and subsequent change. However, there is no relationship between the experience of fear and change; thirty-seven who felt fear changed, whereas ten who felt fear did not change. There is a significant relationship between love and change. Of the 116 who felt love, 109 changed. However, of the 179 who did not feel love, 123 changed.

There are other psychological reasons for change. Survivors of disasters in which others have died are marked by the experience. They may feel guilty ('Why me?') and wonder why they have been singled out for survival. One way of making sense of this is to feel that one's own escape was in some way the work of destiny, that it has personal significance. To come near to death and then escape it must be one of the most profound human experiences, with or without an NDE. Anyone who has ever been in a situation where death seemed imminent or inevitable, but who then survives, feels to some extent reborn. It is as though one has been given a second chance, that one is somehow 'special' to be alive when one might so easily have died.

Almost everyone who has had an NDE finds that he or she has a different perspective on life, and at least one correspondent found this made it hard to be patient with others' seemingly trivial preoccupations and priorities. More commonly, respondents said they felt the experience had made them more caring, and more sympathetic towards others' needs:

> I have never been a particularly religious person . . . or found any answers in religion. But since my NDE I find I have become more sympathetic to other people's problems . . . I try to tell people that life is short and we must all make the best of it that we can . . .

Transformation, however, is by no means universal; 28 per cent

of the people we questioned did not feel the experience changed
them in any significant or permanent way.

12   Faith and the NDE

For a few, the NDE is confirmation of a religious faith they
already have. More usually, it is a spiritual awakening that may
have very little to do with religion in the narrowest sense. Forty-
two per cent reported that they were more spiritual as a result;
22 per cent claimed to be a 'better person', and 40 per cent said
they were more socially conscious than before. The NDE seems,
then, to broaden religious faith rather than simply to confirm it,
leading to a recognition that many paths lead to the same truth.
When the presence of some higher 'Being' is felt, this is only
seldom defined as, for example, a Catholic or a Jewish God.
Christian icons such as Jesus and Mary are only rarely encountered. The experiences have, however, a universal quality. If this
was a purely psychological experience, one would expect it to be
much more culturally influenced than it seems to be.

The NDE certainly tends to confirm belief in some form of
afterlife. Most who have had an NDE have a strong conviction
that some important part of them – their consciousness, their
soul – can exist quite independently of their body, and may
continue to do so after death. It is interesting that only 28 per
cent of the sample said that they would be less likely to commit
suicide after their experience.

Although it is a natural tendency for one to try to interpret a
new experience in the light of one's existing belief system, most
tend not to do this with the NDE. It is much more likely one will
try to modify one's belief system if the experience does not seem
to fit into it. One practising Roman Catholic expressed her own
surprise that her experience did not seem to be related to her
religion.

Had I died, I would most certainly have expected that any visions I
had would have related to my faith, and if I was to see a Being of
Light I would have related it to Jesus or Mary or an Angel. As it was
. . . three Beings appeared to me as young Indian men . . . dressed
alike in high-necked silver coloured tunics with silver turbans on their
heads . . . My whole lifestyle was changed as a result – and I've since

done much reading about various religions and philosophies.

Other respondents expressed a similar view.

> [my experience] . . . hasn't made me more 'religious': what I do feel is that there are so many religions in the world, why should our God be the only one or indeed the correct one? I feel my experience proved there is a God – before that I don't think I really believed in anything, just accepted what my parents believed in.

> I've always believed in life after death, though I no longer belong to any form of organized religion, preferring to find my own path, but if I needed anything to confirm my belief in another plane of existence, that experience certainly did. I feel so grateful to have had it.

> My own belief, and I am not a religious person (I did not believe in an afterlife before this happened), is that we leave this life as easily as passing from one room to another . . . Before my experience I had wondered, like most, about death and, like most, was afraid of the unknown. I now count myself among the privileged in that I now know that there is no pain, there is nothing other than the ending of one chapter and the turning of the page.

13 Psychic gifts

An increase in psychic powers is often reported by those who have had NDEs, and 47 per cent of our sample said they felt the experience had made them more psychically sensitive.

Several said the precognitive ability they acquired was bound up with a 'life preview' experienced during their experience. *Déjà vu* feelings are common. One person reported that he could sometimes anticipate major future occurrences in his life, and explained this by saying,

> It is almost as if, during the near-death experience I saw a speeded-up video of my future life in order to select it or the other. It seems that the odd video frame has been remembered. Similarly I can foresee the future of some people's destiny, but not everyone, just people who seem to have a say in my own.

Strong *déjà vu* feelings, premonitions, an occasional experience of telepathic communication, do, however, occur quite commonly in the general population. The belief that one has healing powers is also quite common. It is difficult to know whether these beliefs are more common amongst those who have had NDEs. It is also possible that those who have psychic experiences or acquire healing abilities after an NDE may in fact have had them prior to the experience, but perhaps have been unaware or have taken no particular notice of them.

There are many reports of people who have developed 'psychic powers' after a head injury. The probability is that these feelings are mediated by the right temporal lobe. A study of seventeen mediums and a group of control subjects found that there was more evidence of brain damage in the mediums, particularly right temporal lobe damage.[10] There does seem to be strong evidence that head injuries may increase a tendency to claim psychic powers, probably because they alter brain function.

The NDE does not simply change a person's attitudes towards death; often it helps one to appreciate life and live it more fully as well.

The effect of my experience has had a profound effect on my life. I thank the Lord for every new day . . .

I am not a particularly religious person, but this experience has totally changed my life . . . I love life and live it to its full. I'm just happy to be allowed to live on this earth for this comparatively short time.

I now feel every day is a new gift to me. Material things are not nearly as important as they used to be and I now look forward with peace and joy to the day of my death . . . Recently someone asked me what I would say if I was told I had to die now. My answer was, 'I'd say, "This is a lovely Now." '

14 Conclusion

The accounts which have been reported in this chapter form a moving testimony to the significance of the near-death experience in the lives of those who have it. Detailed analysis of the accounts leads to a surprising picture of heaven, but a confirming picture of universal love. It is as if the experience of strong and universal emotion is the bedrock of experience upon which is superimposed a partial cognitive and cultural model. This leads to a surprising juxtaposition of images, on the one hand the presence of a Being in a light composed of universal love containing all power and knowledge, on the other a heaven which is notably deficient of content by earthly standards, containing neither harps nor angels.

After analysing all these accounts one is left with the impression that the experiencers were describing exactly what happened to them as accurately as they can. There is a clear indication of a journey by the individual's consciousness, first out of the body and then into the universal and welcoming light. The significance of these experiences to the individual is not in doubt. Scientifically, the experiences cannot be entirely explained by current theories of brain function. Subjectively they indicate both a moral and loving world where care for the individual is paramount.

Notes

1   J. E. Owens, E. W. Cook and I. Stevenson, 'Features of "Near death experience" in relation to whether or not patients were near death', *Lancet*, 336 (November, 1990), 1, 175–6; G. O. Gabbard, S. W. Twemlow and F. C. Jones, 'Do Near Death Experiences occur only near death?', *Journal of Nervous and Mental Diseases*, 169 (1981), 19–27; B. Greyson, 'Near death encounters with and without near-death experiences: comparative NDE scale profiles', *Journal of Near-Death Studies*, 8 (1990), 151–61.

2   B. Greyson, 'The Near-Death Experience Scale', *Journal of Nervous and Mental Diseases*, 171 (6) (1983), 369–75; K. Ring, *Life at Death: A Scientific Investigation of the Near Death Experience* (New York, Coward, 1980).

3   K. Ring and C. K. J. Rosing, 'The Omega Project: an empirical study of the NDE-prone personality', *Journal of Near-Death Studies*, 8 (1990), 211–39.

4   R. Moody, *Life after Life* (Atlanta, Mockingbird, 1975); Ring, *Life at Death*; M. B. Sabom, *Recollection of Death* (London, Corgi, 1982).

5   B. Greyson and N. E. Bush, 'Distressing near-death experiences', *Psychiatry*, 55 (1992), 95–110; Margot Grey, *Return from Death: An Exploration of the Near-Death Experience* (London, Arkana, 1985); M. Rawlings, *Beyond Death's Door* (Nashville, Nelson, 1978).

6   Sabom, *Recollection of Death.*
7   Susan Blackmore, *Dying to Live* (London, Grafton, 1993).
8   R. Noyes and R. Kletti, 'Panoramic memory: a response to the threat of death', *Omega*, 8 (1977), 181–94; R. Noyes and D. Slymen, 'The subjective response to life-threatening danger', *Omega*, 9 (1979), 313–21.
9   M. Morse, *Transformed by the Light* (London, Piatkus, 1992).
10 P. Fenwick, 'Some aspects of the physiology of the mystical experience', in *Psychology*, Survey No. 4, ed. J. Nicholson and B. Foss (Leicester, British Psychological Society, 1983), 203–23.

For a fuller account of the data given here, readers are directed to: Peter and Elizabeth Fenwick, *The Truth in the Light* (London, Headline, 1995).

10
The importance of death in shaping our understanding of life

ANDREW EDGAR

This chapter offers an account of the place that reflection upon death, and specifically upon the inevitable mortality of human beings, has for the interpretation of our lives individually and collectively. The first part of the chapter will be given over to an account of the work of the twentieth-century German philosopher Martin Heidegger. Through consideration of our anxiety before death he attempts to respond to the problem of what it means to be human. It will be suggested that Heidegger's arguments have alarming consequences, in that they undermine the possibility of finding any secure meaning in our lives. Recent developments in sociology allow for a modification of this view. Heidegger's position is seen to express the cultural and institutional inhibitions that distort our experience and understanding of death in contemporary Western society.

1 Heidegger and human nature

At the core of Heidegger's thinking is a vision of what is entailed in being human. Put bluntly, human beings are creatures with bodies, existing in physical, but also social and historical environments. Further, they are unique, and thus separated from other animals, let alone from inanimate objects and plants, in the degree to which they are self-conscious of their own existence. A human being is thus at once an individual who is free to make choices about his or her own life and actions, and a member of a society, and as such is dependent upon the physical, cultural and human resources of the society and world within which he or she lives. This may appear to be an unexceptional description of what it is to be human. It is, sadly, a description that is at odds with much traditional philosophy, and Heidegger quite explicitly sets himself against much of that tradition.

In order to encapsulate the first aspect of what it is to be human, that humans have bodies and live in physical and social environments, Heidegger claims that humans are 'thrown' into the world. The image of throwing is intended to suggest the arbitrariness, not just of our arrival in the world, but also of the world in which we arrive. We no more ask to be born than a stone asks to be thrown into a pond. We have no say as to the body we have (and thus no say on the talents, strengths and abilities our body may allow us), and no say as to the particular society we enter. The society will have existed for a long time before us, and we will make a more or less insignificant mark on its nature and composition. Yet, in contrast, our society makes an incalculable mark upon us. Heidegger's claim is not that humans enter the world ready-formed, with their personalities, beliefs and attitudes intact. While they may have certain innate talents and abilities, people become what they are largely through the impact that their environment has upon them. An individual believes what she does because the beliefs have been learnt and reinforced through experiences in society. Similarly, she will exercise the abilities she does because the opportunities, tools and materials necessary for their development are available in society. Even an athlete becomes an athlete, not simply because of the physical strengths of her body, but because society values and allows the development of that particular form of athleticism. Similarly, a beautiful woman is a beautiful woman only because the culture into which she is thrown values that particular physical appearance.

Heidegger draws out further, rather more surprising consequences, from this account of the embodiment of human beings, concerning the manner in which we come to know our physical and cultural environment. Heidegger wishes to reject any account of knowledge that suggests that we understand the world first and foremost through reflection or contemplation of it. (Such accounts are presupposed in much philosophy.) For Heidegger, knowledge is primarily generated through our activity in the world, and so depends on our having bodies, not just in order to experience that world, but also to manipulate it. We thus understand the world in terms of the instrumental activities, or the 'projects', upon which we are engaged. Indeed, for Heidegger, we take notice of the world only insofar as it is of some practical use to us. 'The wood is a forest of timber, the mountain a quarry of rock; the river is water-power, the wind is wind "in the sails".'[1] A smith thus understands metals, not through abstract reflection upon their chemical composition, but by moulding them in the forge. Similarly his tools are understood not in terms of abstract instructions, but in use.

Theoretical reflection, in science, mathematics and philosophy, is required only when things go wrong. Only when we are frustrated in our projects, when the hammer breaks or the metal fails to bend, do we step back in order to reflect upon the properties of our tools and materials, and so ask why things did not turn out as they usually do. Only then do we reflect upon what our projects really entail, on precisely what it is we expect to get out of them, and thus upon better ways of going about them, or even if it is worth pursuing them at all. Heidegger's contention is, then, that theoretical knowledge is secondary, and occurs in response to, and against a background of, mundane practical activities, taken-for-granted skills and abilities, and unarticulated expectations about how our activities will turn out. Heidegger's reflections upon knowledge will take on deeper significance when he turns to the question of death, for death marks the failure of all projects, and so stimulates the most profound and disquieting reflection of all.

Before turning to the issue of death, the second aspect of Heidegger's view of what it is to be human must be considered. While humans are embodied social creatures, they are also self-conscious and autonomous. A sociological account of humans may lead to the assumption that they are in some way determined by their social environment. Thus it might be thought that what people turn out to be, do or believe will depend wholly upon the particular environments in which they live. Heidegger rejects this implication, because it confuses humanity with any other animate or inanimate thing.

As our knowledge of physics, biology and chemistry improves, we are able to make ever more exact predictions about how objects and systems in the physical world will react and behave.

We know that water will turn from a liquid to a gas at 100 degrees centigrade. We know that a plant will become a bonsai if its roots are carefully clipped. We can also make predictions about human beings based upon biological and medical knowledge of how our bodies react to certain stimuli. As the social sciences become more sophisticated, we might also suppose that we are capable of making predictions about human behaviour under specific social conditions. We know that a human will die if stabbed through the heart, and (perhaps) that unemployment leads to a greater propensity to crime. However, to see human beings as determined by either physical or social properties fails to recognize that they are fundamentally free. Heidegger's point may be summed up so: a causal or deterministic account of human behaviour can never be exhaustive, because nothing can ultimately cause humans to behave in a particular way. Humans may not always recognize it, but they are always free to act differently in all situations.

Heidegger may be taken to be arguing that humans are always capable of acting creatively and unpredictably. While the failure of a project may jolt us out of our complacency, there is always more than one way of proceeding after this jolt. There will always be a range of technical solutions to the problem, as well as reasons that may be called upon to justify the continuation of the project, or to justify its modification or abandonment. The course of action that is chosen will depend upon the way in which the individual involved understands the world and his place within it. Thus, while the forest may indeed be seen as timber, it may also be seen as a source of food or medicines; the mountain may be a quarry or a defence against invasion; the river may be a source of power or a means of transport; and the wind may drive the sails of a ship or a windmill. Similarly, the person may understand himself to be a lumberjack, doctor or soldier. The consequence that Heidegger draws from these reflections is that, while people may be thrown into the world, at some point they must also choose to understand that world and themselves in a certain way. They must select between the competing possibilities provided by their society and by their imaginations, in order to affirm that, at least at this moment, they are indeed doctors and they search the world for medicine, or that they are soldiers and they seek defensible positions and means to deploy their troops. At the heart of Heidegger's philosophy there is the profound paradox that people have an awesome responsibility for a wholly contingent existence.

2 Heidegger and death

The responsibility of our freedom is indeed so awesome that we would much rather forget it. We can, quite easily, proceed by assuming that we have no choice. A forester and a bureaucrat alike can assume that there is no other activity upon which they could be engaged. Soldiers can assume not merely that they must attack the enemy, but that such actions are justified by the most noble values, of defending civilization and even of doing God's work. For Heidegger, such thinking is 'inauthentic'. While it is not necessarily immoral, for it does make life easier, it is mistaken. Such thinking rests upon a mistaken view of what it is to be human, precisely insofar as it ignores our freedom. The experience that forces the individual out of inauthenticity is that of anxiety, and specifically, anxiety before death.

Heidegger is careful to distinguish anxiety from fear. A human may be afraid of something in the world. I might be afraid of tigers, thunderstorms or enemy fire. Anxiety is subtly different. Heidegger suggests that anxiety is not a response to something in the world, but is rather a response to one's very existence, and all that is entailed in being human. The experience is so disquieting (and Heidegger acknowledges that we are typically only aware of anxiety through our attempts to avoid it) precisely because everything encountered in the world is made to appear insignificant. Nothing can any longer provide a ground or motivation for our actions and projects. There is no ultimate reason for bothering to carry on with anything. In the rare and precious experience of anxiety, the world in which the human being usually dwells becomes 'uncanny'. Heidegger's German term is *unheimlich*, which literally means, 'un-home-like'. Anxiety thus strips away all the cosy security of our taken-for-granted, everyday life.

The point of this speculation becomes clearer as anxiety and fear are compared as responses to death. Fear of death is an inauthentic experience. It is to view death as a threat to my continued existence. As such, death comes to be associated with certain things in the world that might be the cause of my death (such as tigers, bullets and cancers). Yet death remains a more or less distant threat in an otherwise secure (and homely) world. Heidegger suggests that inauthentic cultures encourage us to evade confrontation with our own deaths. A phrase such as 'One of these days one will die too', by substituting 'one' for 'I', neatly sidesteps the need to confront death personally. (As the old joke goes: Never say die. Say 'pass on', 'rest in peace' or 'join the choir invisible', but never say 'die'.) We console those who are dying, assuring them that they will not die, and thereby also console ourselves. Ultimately, another's death may be inconvenient, 'if not even a downright tactlessness', although the other person's death assures us that we, at least, are still alive.[2]

An authentic relationship to death does not entail a morbid brooding on our mortality. Rather, it is to recognize the centrality of death to what it means to be human. Death highlights two aspects of human existence. Firstly, only at the moment of death is a person's freedom taken away. Prior to death, a person is never determined by his past, for he can always engage in a new project. While alive, all the projects that we have promised ourselves, from giving up smoking to a holiday in Peru, can still be fulfilled. Even the sinner may repent, so that the sins become the exception rather than the rule of his life. At death, all these possibilities cease. Death thus highlights the freedom of the living.

Secondly, one's death is always, unavoidably, one's own. For all other activities that I carry out during my life, I could, in principle, be represented by someone else. Someone else could write this chapter for me, live in my house, and so on. I must, however, die my own death. But further, death is always my own, because, at the moment of death I become aware that the resources and inhabitants of the social world will 'fail me'. Macquarrie suggests that Christ's parable of a rich man storing up his wealth in newly enlarged barns, corresponds, at least in part, to Heidegger's point.[3] Although Heidegger may concur that our existence should be judged by more than the mere accumulation of personal wealth or the achievement of worldly reputation and status, he is not obviously seeking to direct us towards spiritual, or other-worldly, rewards. Rather, he observes that at the moment of death all the worldly projects that have sustained us, and given meaning and purpose to our existence, crumble to nothing. Death marks the ultimate failure of any project on which a person might be engaged. In consequence, the clear-sighted anticipation of death stimulates the most profound reflection, resulting in the stripping away of every taken-for-granted presupposition of worth or value that I might have used to justify my existence. An authentic existence is freed of any background assumptions or illusions about the worth of our activities and projects. The fact that somebody continues in a particular project or action ultimately depends wholly upon the choice of that person.

Such clear-sightedness amounts, for Heidegger, to our choosing death. In this superficially bizarre claim, Heidegger is not advocating suicide. That would entail the reduction of death to a contingent possibility of human existence, alongside all the other activities that a person could undertake. The point is that while the precise moment of our death is indefinite, that it will occur is certain. The choice of death thereby entails accepting the fact that the very nature of our existence is characterized by death (and thus by our freedom and individual responsibility). If human beings are necessarily embodied, then they are also necessarily mortal. The inauthentic pretence that the world is benign or homely is thereby shattered. The world cannot be benign, for to live in this world entails our being destroyed by it. Hence, we should not fear particular things that we encounter in the world, as if they constituted some distinctive and finite collection of mortal threats. We should rather experience anxiety at the uncanny, for the threat comes not from a few menacing items in an otherwise benign world, but from the very fact that we are part of a world that is characterized by mortality and transience.

Macquarrie suggests that Heidegger's philosophy delivers us from the illusions of inauthentic existence, only to offer 'an open-eyed despair'.[4] Death gives meaning to human existence only by revealing what Heidegger calls its 'structure', which is to say, the preconditions of what it is to be human. It cannot, however, give meaning in the sense of fulfilment. The implication of Heidegger's account is that the individual who dies content in the achievements and purposes of her life is ultimately deluded, and has done nothing more than appease an inauthentic society.

3   The sociology of death

Heidegger provides a stimulating view of what it is to be human, reflecting profoundly upon both the social aspects of human existence and the individual's scope for autonomy. However, his account of anxiety before death, and its consequences in the recognition of the ungrounded nature of our existence, is intuitively problematic. In this section, an attempt will be made to construct a more positive view of the role that reflection upon death plays in giving meaning and coherence to our lives, by considering some recent developments in the sociology of death. Specifically, it will be suggested that Heidegger pays too little attention to the social and historical nature of human existence. While he recognizes the need to understand human existence in socio-historical terms, there is little concrete analysis, so that many of his comments on society are naive or superficial.

While agreeing with Heidegger's premise that humans are uniquely creatures that are aware of their mortality, Norbert Elias is at pains to point out that this awareness is itself due to human culture: 'It is variable and group-specific; no matter how natural and immutable it seems to the members of each particular society, it has been learned.'[5] Yet, it has also been argued that while society makes us aware of our mortality, that very awareness poses a threat to the society. Anthony Giddens, working within a Heideggerian framework, argues that on an everyday basis, people in society take for granted the coherence and worth of their activities. This coherence and meaning is, however, fragile, and can be easily overwhelmed by events that remain outside the control of the society. Such events include major and life-threatening ones, such as natural disasters or threats of invasion. Death is the paradigm form of disruption, because it most vividly and irreversibly demonstrates the limits of the society's power to guarantee the security of its members. This failure must be explained, excused or hidden, at pain of losing the individual's continued trust in (and thus commitment to) the existing social order.[6] In consequence, the richness and depth of a society's culture and technology represent, at least in part, that society's attempt to cope with and excuse the deaths of its members.

Zygmunt Bauman has developed this approach by suggesting

that within any given society certain 'survival policies' will be accepted and sustained as part of the dominant culture. A survival policy is a means 'to channel the horror of death (and thus to organize the individual's concern with survival)' so that it serves to maintain the stability of the society to which the individual belongs.[7] Bauman offers brief analyses of four such survival policies. Firstly, a belief in God explains mortality in terms of the inscrutability of divine providence. A promise of survival beyond the death of the body shifts a person's attention away from the body, the fate of which cannot be controlled, towards thoughts and actions that are under voluntary control. Secondly, with the development of modern science and rational doubt in the Enlightenment, the other-worldly and therefore untestable claims of religions come under suspicion. They are replaced by a secular commitment to the improvement of the living conditions of the community. Suffering and death are thus justified as challenges to be overcome, or trials that have to be passed through, in order to achieve a glorious future for one's fellows. Nationalism, communism and fascism provide examples of this policy. Thirdly, in an increasingly private and individualistic society, survival is sought in the love between two people. Individuals seek an ideal relationship that will transcend the finitude of their bodily existence. The impossibility of this demand leads to excessive expectations being placed on personal relationships. Finally, Bauman suggests that in contemporary Western societies 'regimes of self-care' are dominant. These involve a renewed focus upon the individual's body. On the one hand, the individual tries to transcend the limits of the body, not by postponing death or by envisaging some form of survival outside the body, but through increasing the body's performance (typically in some form of athleticism). The limitations are therefore transcended in momentary peaks of physical achievement. On the other hand, fear of death is displaced by a preoccupation with health, thereby facilitating an active engagement with specific causes of death, such as heart disease, cancer or stress, by changing one's diet or by undertaking rigorous exercise routines.

Bauman notes that the success of such policies will depend upon the type of society in which they are used, and thus upon the availability of appropriate physical and cultural resources. Philip Mellor, following Giddens, offers an analysis of the experience of death in contemporary Western society that complements Bauman's outline. Mellor's account begins by noting that modern culture offers a proliferation of explanations and justifications for death.[8] Within a multicultural society, all four of Bauman's survival policies, and more, will coexist. While some may be more widely accepted than others, none will have complete dominance. Precisely because no single account can be accepted without question, no one can rest secure in his or her beliefs. The religious believer, for example, will be continually assaulted by the scepticism of a secular world; the nationalist or communist is confronted by the tragic failure of both causes in the twentieth century. In Heideggerian terms, the individual cannot then merely rest in the innocent security of inauthenticity. The projects that might make sense of death are continually threatened, and thus require continual reflection (or a stubborn short-sightedness) in order to remain plausible. It is thus within a multicultural society that the individual comes to bear a deeper responsibility for his or her beliefs.

The lack of a single account of death serves to increase the threat that death poses to the social order. For Giddens, multicultural societies thus deal with death primarily through its active concealment. In contemporary society, death and the process of dying are removed from everyday and public experience. Elias describes this so:

> Parents in [modern] societies are often more reticent than earlier in talking to their children about death and dying. Children can grow up without ever having seen a dead body. At earlier stages of development the sight of corpses was usually far more commonplace.[9]

Giddens notes that even the handling of capital punishment follows this path of increased exclusion from public view. Similarly, in medical practice the dying are physically removed to hospitals and hospices. Yet this process of concealment cannot be wholly successful, precisely because it places a greater burden on the individual to cope with death and bereavement when they finally have to be faced. A lack of familiarity with death leaves the survivor at a loss how to behave towards the dying. Even the rituals of the funeral have become unfamiliar, and thus increasingly demanding. Bauman's policy of self-care thus provides a reasonable (if short-sighted) response to this problem. Lacking any socially acquired abilities to articulate our anxiety before death, or at least having this ability only in the context of continual doubt and questioning, we avoid death in favour of a concern with physical performance and health.

These sociological analyses may now be used in a reconsideration of Heidegger. It has been suggested above that Heidegger's account is ultimately insufficiently sociological. At the crux of his argument is the claim that the community and the material world fail us at the moment of death. This was interpreted in terms of Macquarrie's appeal to the parable of the rich man storing up material wealth. On this level, Heidegger's point is acceptable. However, the very existence of survival policies suggests, at a different level, that the social world does not leave us alone at death. On the contrary, a culture is capable of providing us with rich resources in order to make sense of our death. It may be suggested that just as humans are constituted as living beings by their communities, they are also constituted as beings who can die. (Indeed, given the threat that death poses to society, such constitution is necessary for the continued stability of society.) Death is no more a brute fact of existence than is anything else in a culturally interpreted world. The failure of contemporary society is less due to an inability to help, as Heidegger argues, than to an active withdrawal of help. Heidegger's account of the way in which inauthentic society provides us with the means to avoid talking about and confronting death is clearly echoed in the accounts of Giddens, Mellor and Elias. Yet Giddens and Mellor, especially, suggest that this is not an escape route offered to the fearful, but the active concealment of a failing of contemporary society. The living are physically excluded from the presence of the dead and dying, and are denied the language to express their feelings or their support for the dying, precisely because there are no longer the cultural resources available that will allow most people to feel secure in the face of death. The groundlessness of my existence, that is exposed in authenticity, is not then simply given as Heidegger supposes, but is rather generated by a particular type of society.

Heidegger need not deny all of this. He need only observe that the resources provided by a culture to make sense of death are indicative of an inauthentic stance towards death. For an individual to look to his society to provide a cast-iron explanation of death is a sign of inauthenticity. Bauman implicitly acknowledges the inauthenticity of survival policies, noting that 'the search for a foolproof . . . policy of survival is itself a ruse – a conspiracy of silence about the ultimate futility of effort, to bury the truth that the ostensible purpose of the search cannot be reached.'[10] Mellor's account is, however, even more significant. The background of doubt that lies behind all personally adopted survival policies in a modern pluralist society suggests, paradoxically, that some state akin to authenticity is becoming unavoidable. The individual cannot but be aware that his or her survival policy may be flawed, and that it cannot be rigorously defended. It may be noted of the two strategies that Bauman describes under the policy of self-care, that concern with one's health is an epitome of inauthenticity. A concern with physical performance, however, engages with the limitations of one's body (and thus the contingency of one's bodily existence and one's inevitable mortality) and does not try to cheat death. As such, it has every indication of being authentic.

Yet, as Giddens has argued, the individual's increasing awareness of the fragility of her survival policies is compromised by the development of social institutions that serve to conceal death. Paradoxically, inauthenticity may no longer be chosen as a means of escape by the individual, but is rather enforced on a routine basis due to the lack of opportunity to witness death or dying, and by the withdrawal of resources that allow people to articulate or anticipate their experiences of death. A more social conception of human being than that offered by Heidegger thus allows the suggestion that inauthenticity is not a fault of, or even an option for, the individual , but is rather a fault of the community within which he or she lives. Whatever motivation a person might have to live authentically, that motivation will come to nothing if his community removes the possibility of the appropriate experience of death. Again, as Elias remarks, human awareness of death is always shaped by a particular culture. This point is given renewed significance by Bauman. He notes that death is not merely a threat to social stability *per se*, but more specifically to reason. This does not merely indicate the problems encountered in providing a coherent account of death, but rather, as Heidegger argues, in the part played by death as the ultimate mark of failure of all projects. Death thereby exposes the futility of all instrumental reason.[11] The achievement of any goal is ultimately transitory. Mellor takes this point further.[12] Modern Western cultures depend upon the successful use of instrumental reason in the control of the physical and social environment through science, technology and social administration. Modern cultures may therefore be seen to share a fundamental concern with the subordination of nature to human ends. Insofar as death marks the limit of this control, it poses a threat to any modern culture, and thus to any culture that encourages its members to think and to understand themselves and their world in primarily instrumental terms. While Heidegger, especially in his later writings, is critical of modern technology, his interpretation of human existence in terms of an engagement in instrumental projects shares much with modern culture. Again, Heidegger appears as a mirror of his time. It may then be suggested that the 'clear-eyed despair' that he offers his readers should lead not to the abandonment of any attempt to find meaning in death, or to use our confrontation with death to give substance to our lives. It rather serves to make us aware of the inhibitions that contemporary society places in the way of such understanding.

Notes

1 Martin Heidegger, *Being and Time* (Oxford, Blackwell, 1962), 40–1.
2 Heidegger, *Being and Time*, 297–8.
3 John Macquarrie, *An Existentialist Theology* (London, SCM, 1973), 114.
4 Ibid., 119.
5 Norbert Elias, *The Loneliness of the Dying* (Oxford, Blackwell, 1985), 4–5.
6 Anthony Giddens, *Modernity and Self-identity* (Cambridge, Polity, 1991).
7 Zygmunt Bauman, 'Survival as a social construct', in Mike Featherstone (ed.), *Cultural Theory and Cultural Change* (London, Sage, 1992), 13.
8 Philip A. Mellor, 'Death in high modernity: the contemporary presence and absence of death', in David Clark (ed.), *The Sociology of Death: Theory, Culture, Practice* (Oxford, Blackwell, and The Sociological Review, 1993), 11–30, at 18–19.

9   Elias, op. cit., 85.
10 Bauman, 'Survival', 21.
11 Ibid., 1 and 5.
12 Mellor, op. cit., 25.

11
Life and death in the light of an eternal hope

PAUL BADHAM

1 The meaning of life in a secular context

From a secular perspective life has no meaning or purpose other than the goals we set ourselves as individuals or as members of a community. Death, understood as a final end, marks the terminus of our brief existence on this tiny planet. Life must therefore be sacred to each one of us, for it is only in the few years we have on earth that we are to live and move and have our being. According to Ecclesiastes (the only secular thinker to have his work included in the Bible), all is ultimately empty and therefore 'there is nothing good for anyone except to be happy and live the best life he can while he is alive . . . it is good and proper for a man to eat and drink and enjoy himself in return for his labours . . . to enjoy life with a woman . . . and whatever task lies in hand to do it with all your might because in the grave to which you are heading there is neither doing nor thinking.'[1] Ecclesiastes is often thought of as cynical or pessimistic and many Christians have questioned how his work ever came to be included in the Hebrew Bible. But from a secular perspective, his philosophy of life is a realistic recognition of what it means to be human, and his denial of any ultimate purpose is always linked with a description of how we can find satisfaction and dignity in accepting the limits of our finitude.

2 The religious vision of life

From the perspective of the world's great religions the human situation is very different. In Judaism, Christianity and Islam, human life is precious because these religions hold that human life is ultimately the creation of an all-powerful and all-loving God who wills to enter a relationship with us and whose loving purposes cannot be defeated by death. In this theistic context human life is seen in cosmic perspective, and life is seen as having enormous significance and meaning as the first stage on our journey towards God. In Hinduism and Buddhism the meaning of life is seen differently as one of many lives we shall pass through until our absorption into the absolute, or our entry into the deathless state of parinirvana.[2] But in both cases our present life has cosmic significance in that what we do now shapes the Karma which will determine our destiny beyond the grave.

There is therefore a fundamental difference between a purely naturalistic world view, in which this life is all there is, and a religious world view, in which this life finds it true meaning against the backdrop of eternity. This change in perspective may not necessarily make a dramatic impact on how we actually live. In their journey through life a mortalist and a survivalist may both face the same kind of experiences and challenges, and respond in similar ways to them. Most of our thinking and planning is directed to relatively short-term goals, and even our long-term thinking – for example about our careers, house purchase or pension planning tends to stop at the horizon of our retirement. It is also the case, as we shall see later, that what the world religions teach as to the kind of behaviour which best helps us fashion ourselves in readiness for eternity is not, at least for the layman, very different from a humanist vision as to the best way for us to live authentically in the present.

There is of course one great difference in that the theistic believer feels conscious of the presence of God and will seek to acknowledge God's lordship in worship and prayer. Similarly the non-theistic religious person, such as the Advaita Hindu or the Theravada Buddhist will practise meditation and mindfulness and will consciously avoid the domination of human desires and passions. So religious convictions do change behaviour in ways the believer regards as important, but even more significantly they change the perspective in which what happens to one is understood. And this different perspective becomes particularly important as we come to face death.

3 Death as the central point of division between a naturalist and religious viewpoint

Death is the point where the naturalistic and the religious visions of what life is about diverge most sharply. For the one, death means extinction, the final ending of our personal existence. For the other, death marks a division between our present mode of life, and a future and hopefully better one. Sometimes of course this sharp distinction is blurred, because some who profess religious belief reinterpret religious language in a wholly secular manner, while a few who reject religious belief continue to hope for some kind of personal continuance through death. What is even more common is that many who nominally affirm a future hope have no lively expectation of its realization. Such a state is particularly common today where many committed Christians suffer considerable 'cognitive dissonance' through an awareness of how their beliefs differ from the secular assumptions which dominate most informed discussion, and condition the behaviour of most medical practitioners towards their dying patients.

However, in a truly pluralist society it is wrong that one paradigm should hold sway. Given that something like 38 per cent of the population of Britain (and 70 per cent of Americans) believe in life after death,[3] it does seem appropriate in an academic discussion to explore life and death from the perspective of an eternal hope, and consider how the possession of such hope might affect the person facing death and those seeking to minister to the dying believer.

4 Belief in a creator God

The foundational theistic belief shared by Jews, Christians and Muslims is that the universe was created by an all-powerful and all-loving God as the context in which sentient, rational life could emerge and could come freely into fellowship with God. The greatest problem facing such a vision is the fact that the world contains much evil and if human life is considered as totally extinguished at death, there would appear to be no way in which such evil could be in any sense explained or accounted for. Hence belief in God is wholly dependent on supposing that God can overcome the power of death. Hence belief in God and belief in life after death are two mutually interdependent doctrines. Let us explore this by looking more deeply into the problem of evil and Christian responses to it.

5 The 'problem of evil' within Christianity

The fact that evil and suffering undoubtedly exist poses a challenge to the Christian supposition that this world was created by an all-powerful, all-knowing and all-benevolent God. Either he cannot abolish evil, in which case he is not all-powerful, or he chooses not to, and cannot therefore be all-benevolent. Many attempts have been made to meet this challenge. Process theology suggests that God is not all-powerful. The so-called Christian Science sect sees evil as an illusion. Traditional theology explains evil as the product of the 'fall' of the first man and woman. Popular piety suggests that though the problem cannot be resolved philosophically, it was resolved religiously in the Crucifixion of Christ perceived as God incarnate, identifying with and sharing in the depths of our suffering. But serious problems face all these 'solutions'. To deny either the competence of God to end suffering or the existence of evil seems an evasion of the issue. A historical fall is too much at variance with the discoveries of archaeology, anthropology and evolutionary history to be a live option. And I have never understood how the problem of evil is supposed to be helped by the notion that God also experiences it. We welcome the sympathy of friends who we know are powerless to help us. But we would feel mocked by expressions of concern from those who had it comfortably in their power to save us but chose not to do so. The problem of evil is certainly not solved by saying that God chooses to suffer with us rather than rescue us from our plight.

Some philosophers have put forward the so-called 'free-will defence' which argues that the possibility of evil and the existence of an objective world with stable laws of nature are necessary for the emergence of free and responsible agents. This view forms an important part of the 'soul-making' theodicy, and although it can to a certain extent stand on its own I shall consider it simply as part of the wider thesis. For if the free responsible agents who are created through their interaction with the stable environment face a future terminated by suffering, disease, death and extinction, then the question of why God allows evil remains unanswered. Hence the free-will defence needs the wider perspective of the soul-making theodicy.

6 The soul-making theodicy

The soul-making theodicy fully accepts that, looking at life simply from within the transitory limits of human existence, the case against belief that the world was created by a wholly benevolent, all-powerful and all-knowing God is overwhelming. This world is not a hedonist's paradise. It is a struggle for existence where we earn our bread by the sweat of our brow. We face innumerable challenges, hardships and difficulties. Ultimately we will age and die, unless we experience premature death through accident, microbe or virus. But the Christian perspective is not confined to this life only. If it were so confined, Christians would, according to St Paul be 'of all people most to be pitied.'[4]

However, from its foundation, Christianity has been a religion committed to belief in heaven, a divine kingdom in which sorrowing and sighing have no place, and in which God becomes the most central feature of our experiencing. Yet Christians have always intuited that such a world could only be appreciated and experienced by fully formed persons. We have to become 'fitted' for heaven by what we do here. Free responsible beings cannot simply be created by divine fiat. Rather we develop our characters and personalities through facing up to the difficulties and challenges of life, and thereby become persons capable of an eternal relationship with God. John Hick expresses the principle behind this concept thus:

> Virtues formed within the agent as a hard-won deposit of his own right decisions in situations of challenge and temptation are intrinsically more valuable than virtues created within him ready made and without any effort on his part... If God's purpose was to create finite persons embodying the most valuable kind of moral goodness, he would have to create them, not as already perfect beings but rather as imperfect creatures who can then attain to the more valuable kind of goodness through their own free choices.[5]

This way of thinking was classically articulated by the poet John

Keats when he wrote to his brother and sister in April 1819, 'Do you not see how necessary a world of pains and troubles is to school an intelligence and make it a Soul? . . . Call the World if you please "The Vale of Soul-making".'[6] In this schema we shape our personhood by the way we engage with the responsibilities and duties we face in the everyday tasks of life in a world subject to natural laws, where what we do or fail to do has consequences. It is no part of the soul-making theodicy that suffering in itself is ennobling or character-forming, for there would be very strong evidence against so simplistic a view. But what the theodicy does say is that a real objective physical world, governed by regular physical laws, provides an environment more suited to the development of responsible agents than would an environment in which divine intervention saved humanity from the consequences of its folly, or from the heart-ache and challenge implicit in any finite and physical existence.

After personhood has been fully formed, then, it may well be that life in a heaven of eternal rest, and peace and bliss would become conceivable. But it could only be appreciated and experienced by those who have first undergone the person-forming experience available to us in this world. Moreover it is likely that we may need to undergo further growth in a life after death. John Hick envisages many lives in many worlds,[7] and this view has many antecedents in earlier Christian writings. Within Catholicism there is the tradition of purgatory, and many Protestants talk of an intermediate state. Hence the soul-making theodicy is not required to suppose that the necessary growth is completed within this life. It merely claims that this life provides a good environment for spiritual growth which may well need further development beyond the grave as the person journeys into God.

It is integral to this view that our 'soul', character or identity as persons is not something we come into the world with. We shape our personhood by the way we live and in response to the challenges and stimuli of life. From a philosophical standpoint, this view requires a concept of soul as an emergent property. Any view of the soul which takes serious note of modern genetics and neurophysiology has to accept that the soul is shaped and influenced by the way our brains and bodies develop and are moulded by the experiences of life and our responses to them.

Consequently I see talk of a 'soul-making' theodicy as literally descriptive language of how our identity is shaped. Clearly this identity is shaped in and through our bodily existence, but Christians believe that the ultimate destiny of this subject will transcend this existence. Keith Ward expresses this larger vision well:

> God is the true end of the soul, and in this sense, its goal, its proper purpose and true nature, lies beyond the physical universe. That is a strong reason for thinking that the subject which is embodied in this world may properly find other forms of experience and action , in contexts lying beyond this universe . . .Of course the soul depends on the brain . . . but the soul need not always depend on the brain, any more than a man need always depend on the womb which supported his life before birth.[8]

7 The meaning of life and death in Judaism

Judaism began as a wholly 'this-world' faith. It was in the here and now that God was related to his people, and the world of the dead was outside God's dominion. At an early stage some Jews appear to have believed in some vague shadowy kind of survival in a place called Sheol, rather like the Homeric picture of Hades. But as time went by Sheol becomes increasingly equivalent to 'the Grave', in which it is assumed that people cease to exist. 'We must all die. We are like water spilt on the ground which cannot be gathered up again.' 'Man will perish for ever like his own dung.' He is 'of dust and will return to dust'. In the grave he will rot away, 'with maggots beneath him and worms on top.'[9] This view was reconciled with belief in a loving God in two ways: first by assuming that God's primary relationship was with the nation rather than the individual, and second by the assumption that God showed his concern for the individual by rewarding the virtuous with long life and prosperity and punishing the wicked with earthly disaster.

Both assumptions came increasingly to be questioned. Old Testament psalms and proverbs constantly raise the issue 'Why do the righteous suffer?' The fullest discussion occurs in the Book of Job, which eventually concludes that the only possible response is to accept that human beings have no right to question the ways of God, but must simply acknowledge his divine wisdom.[10] But the inadequacy of such a response became apparent during the persecution of Antiochus Epiphanes, the first of the devastating persecutions to which the Jews have been subject throughout history when thousands of the most faithful perished. Faced with such a disaster both to righteous individuals and to the nation as a whole, the only way belief in God's love could remain credible was to affirm faith in the power of God to raise up the dead. In our day, the Holocaust has had a comparable effect, leading some Jews to feel that belief in God's goodness is no longer possible, and that, to use Stendhal's epigram, 'The only excuse for God is that he does not exist.' But for those whose faith has held, a belief in a life after death has been re-emphasized as an essential component of an intelligible faith. Rabbi Cohn Sherbok writes: 'The belief in the Hereafter has helped Jews make sense of the world as a creation of a good and all-powerful God and provided a source of great consolation for their travail on earth.' Without such a belief Jews would 'face great difficulties reconciling the belief in a providential God who watches over his chosen people with the terrible events of modern Jewish history.'[11] On this view, belief in a future life became an essential component of an intelligible understanding of Jewish belief in God, both because of the problem of evil and also for the fulfilment of the life of the righteous individual, for (as Cohn Sherbok makes clear) the 'qualification for entrance to heaven (Gan Eden) is to lead a good life in accordance with God's laws.'[12] Life therefore has meaning for both the individual and the community because it is directed towards the transcendent goal of the kingdom of God.

8 The meaning of life and death in Islam

Islam shares with Judaism and Christianity the belief in an all-powerful, all-knowing and all-compassionate creator God. Consequently, from a philosophical standpoint, the existence of evil is as much a challenge in Islam as in the other Abrahamic faiths. Religiously, however, the issue is far less pressing. A key requirement for one to be a good Muslim is an attitude of submission (Islam) to what God has determined. Hence to question what God has done, or to feel a need to 'justify' God in the face of evil indicates a non-submissive, non-Islamic attitude. On the other hand, if the problem is raised as an issue by a non-Muslim, a defence of God's ways can certainly be permitted. In constructing such a defence, a Muslim would take for granted that the frame of reference would include the Hereafter (Al-Akhirah). There is scarcely a chapter in the Qur'ān which does not refer to the Hereafter, and in the book as a whole there are no fewer than 113 references to it. As Sulayman Nyang argues, 'It is necessary to see the belief in a future life as integrally related to the total Islamic view of life in the Sublunar world including man's role in this world and the significance of his faith.'[13] The Qur'ān makes clear that man was not created for sport, but has a serious mission to undertake.[14]

In the Islamic tradition, our life in this sublunar world is explicitly seen as a preparation for the Hereafter. We will ultimately be accountable to God for the way we have lived, so what we do matters because it shapes the persons we become. The distinguished Islamic theologian Salih Tug expresses the matter thus:

> Just as from dust man has evolved, from the deeds he does the higher man is evolved . . . The human frame is only a vehicle by which the soul must develop itself. The soul has to evolve by its own effort from the crude form of simple consciousness to a certain stage of spiritual development . . . Our present life is a preparation. It is necessary to bring out our faculties and raise them to a certain stage of evolution during our earthly sojourn. Then alone shall we be fit for progress in the life after death . . . but we can enter that life only if we have made ourselves fit for it in our physical lifetime.[15]

This seems a clear endorsement of the view that the meaning of this life is to be understood in the context of a 'soul-making' theodicy.

9   The meaning of life and death in Buddhism

The starting point for all Buddhist thought is the recognition that suffering exists. The reality of suffering in this life is the essential presupposition of each of the Four Noble Truths from which the Buddhist philosophy of life derives. Moreover Buddhism does not believe in a creator God whose ways need to be 'justified', nor does it think in categories of a 'soul' which needs to be 'made'. At first sight, therefore, it might seem that the Buddhist approach to life and death was very different from that of the three Abrahamic religions we have so far considered. However, if we look more closely into the Buddha's teaching we may find that the underlying attitude to life and death is more similar to that of the other religions than might at first sight appear to be the case.

The Buddha was totally clear that to seek fulfilment through a materialistic or hedonistic approach to life was thoroughly misguided. Old age, disease and death will bring to naught all worldly hopes. The Buddha's primary response to the reality of suffering was to teach us to overcome our fear of the unsatisfactoriness, suffering or *dukkha* of life by recognizing the transience and impermanence or *annica* of all things. He believed that if we really understood our situation, and achieved true 'enlightenment' about the nature of reality, we would not attach our sense of identity or our search for meaning to anything as transitory and insubstantial as our present experience of selfhood or the fleeting desires which flow from our sensory awareness in the present. Much of the Buddha's teaching is essentially concerned with helping people to cope with suffering in the here and now by having a truer insight into the reality of the human situation. This has led many to interpret the original Buddhist message as essentially practical and down to earth, and as unconcerned about the nature of any supposed future life, concerning which, having no reliable knowledge, we enter instead into a wilderness of speculation which the Buddha urged us to avoid.

However it is mistaken to suppose that the Buddha's thought was limited to this life alone. As Edward Conze points out in his preface to the section of his edition of Buddhist scriptures which deals with other worlds, 'The horizon of Buddhism is not bounded by the limits of the sensory world, their true interests lie beyond it.'[16] The Buddha himself saw human life within a cosmic perspective in which we pass through a succession of lives on our onward journey towards enlightenment. The ultimate deathless state of Nirvana will be reached only when we transcend the cycle of rebirth, and finally rise above the self-centredness of our present condition.

10 What the Buddha meant by his 'no-self' doctrine

One of the most basic Buddhist beliefs is the doctrine of *Anatta*, usually translated as the 'no-self' doctrine and interpreted as a total repudiation of the concept of the soul. However, every denial has to be understood in relation to what is being denied. The Buddha made it absolutely clear that what he opposed was the Hindu notion of a soul or *atman* as an eternal, unchanging essence, existing independently of others, unaffected by the traumas of life and proceeding through a succession of lives. This *atman* should ideally be unaffected by the claims of our fleshly nature, and ascetic practices and an ideal of keeping apart from society have evolved to aid this independence. This picture of an immortal changeless self at the heart of our being was anathema to the Buddha. 'The speculative view that . . . I shall be atman after death, permanent, abiding, everlasting, unchanging, and that I shall exist as such for eternity', is not that wholly and completely foolish.[17] It seems to me that the Buddha was absolutely right in his denial. Modern philosophy of mind has increasingly moved in the direction pioneered by the Buddha over 2,000 years ago. For example, Derek Parfit's influential work *Reasons and Persons* concludes with a chapter on the Buddha's views.[18] It has become increasingly clear that we cannot identify ourselves with an unchanging self. But, as John Hick has pointed out, it is not realistic to argue 'no immutable, eternal, independent self, therefore no self.'[19] In the soul-making hypothesis it is axiomatic that there is no unchanging soul, but rather that we are constantly changing and developing as we respond to the challenges and stimuli of life. Only a dynamic concept of selfhood does justice to experience or empirical reality. It seems to me, therefore, that there is no necessary clash between a soul-making theodicy and the no-self doctrine when we examine the terminology of both theories critically. Both repudiate an unchanging selfhood, and both affirm that what we become is the product of what we do. Ironically, therefore, I would argue that in real terms there are greater problems with fitting Hinduism into a soul-making theodicy than Buddhism. For though Hinduism undoubtedly attaches great importance to the soul (*atman*) yet the picture of it as an unchanging entity raises fundamental problems. However, if we move on to consider the concept of Karma in both Hinduism and Buddhism we may move towards a resolution of this difficulty.

11 Theodicy and Karma: the Hindu and Buddhist understanding of life

Neither Hinduism nor Buddhism is concerned with a human relationship with a creator God, which lies at the heart of belief in a future life in the Judaeo–Christian–Islamic traditions. However, both are concerned with belief in a moral order underlying all things, which finds expression in the doctrine of Karma. The essence of the law of Karma is that what we are is the product of what we have been, and what we shall be depends on what we do now. Historically this doctrine was shaped in a context of belief in rebirth or reincarnation, leading through a succession of lives to the ultimate goal of being one with the ultimate (*moksha*) or entering the deathless state of *Nirvana*. Hence, our behaviour in this life has cosmic significance and meaning, since it determines our future destiny. I suggest that this doctrine is, in its practical effect, analogous to the soul-making theodicy in the three theistic religions we have discussed. Both doctrines see life as having significance within a wider frame of reference than this life alone, and both possess a keen commitment to an underlying moral order, so that what we do matters, whether 'to fit us for heaven' or to fulfil our karmic destiny. In each religion, the ultimate goal which gives significance and meaning to our striving is a transcendent one. In Judaism, Christianity and Islam it is to find our ultimate destiny in the Hereafter with God. In Buddhism it is to achieve the deathless state of *Nirvana*, and in Hinduism ultimately the hope is that we achieve liberation or *moksha* from the cycle of reincarnation. In all cases, the ways in which we respond to the challenges of life in this world are the means whereby we shape our personhood or create and fulfil our Karma, and hence grow more towards what we ought to be.

12 Affirming this world also

It is frequently suggested that belief in a transcendent destiny leads people to despise this world or take it less than seriously.

This can of course sometimes happen, and world renunciation is
to be found in many religious traditions. But the central thrust of
any soul-making theodicy or any doctrine of Karma is to affirm
the importance of what we do now. For although what the religions teach is directed towards the fulfilment of a transcendent
destiny, what is actually prescribed for our everyday life on earth
is, at least for the lay person, the conscientious fulfilment of the
duties and obligations of everyday life. Saints in all three theistic
traditions have warned against the idea that one ought to do good
in order to win heaven. Rather, virtuous actions should be done
for their own sake, because they are themselves good and
contribute to the well-being of the individual and society in the
here and now. If God is perceived to be a loving and good creator
one ought to be able to conclude that creation is for the benefit
of the creature. Consequently, exploring what is 'natural' to
humanity becomes an appropriate basis for moral judgement,
and attending to what can be shown empirically to enhance
human fulfilment is likewise legitimate. Hence although there is
often in practice a clash between the ethical thinking of ecclesias-
tical hierarchs and secular thinkers, in principle such clashes
should not occur. As Grotius argued long ago, a true natural-law
ethic ought to be capable of being worked out 'etsi Deus non
daretur' (as if God were not a premise).[20] Likewise, if we turn to
Buddhism to exemplify the religious wisdom of the East, we note
that the way the householder (as distinct from the monk) can
obtain good Karma is to follow the basic ethical principles of the
Dharma and fulfil all one's obligations to family and society. In
practical terms, the behaviour necessary for becoming 'fitted for
heaven' or 'fulfilling one's Karma' is also the behaviour best
suited to the full realization of one's potential as a human person.

13   The practical implications of seeing life and death in the light of an eternal hope

If we believe that what we do matters because it shapes what we
become we will tend to have a positive attitude towards the challenges of life. These are the means by which we grow and
develop. Thus, at each different stage of life, one would seek to
throw oneself into the tasks and duties appropriate to it. A
conscientious person will take education seriously in youth, not

simply in terms of academic achievement but hopefully the all-round challenge of nurturing whatever talents one has. These may include the development of athletic, musical, aesthetic or organizational abilities, as well as simply intellectual. Then one may move on to the tasks entailed by one's job or profession, and perhaps also take on additional civic or social concerns. For many there will come family responsibilities and the cares and responsibilities of bringing up children or caring for aged parents. For some there may be office in a voluntary society, pressure group, cultural or political organization or church. All these things may provide people with a feeling of meaning to their individual lives and give them their sense of worth and dignity. Such a positive attitude to life is a good in itself and from a humanist perspective might be self-chosen as a way to attribute meaning to one's daily activity. But from a religious perspective the meaning is all the richer for being set in a cosmic framework leading onwards to the fullness of life in the world beyond.

Notes

1   Ecclesiastes 3:12, 5:18, 9:9.
2   For documentation of this see Paul and Linda Badham, *Death and Immortality in the Religions of the World* (New York, Paragon House, 1987) and Paul Badham, 'Death and immortality: towards a global synthesis', in D. Cohn Sherbok and C. Lewis, *Beyond Death* (London, Macmillan, 1994).
3   Anton Van der Walle, *From Darkness to the Dawn* (London, SCM, 1984), 11.
4   1 Corinthians 15:19.
5   John Hick, 'An Irenaean theodicy', in Paul Badham, *A John Hick Reader* (London, Macmillan, 1991), 94.
6   M. B. Forman (ed.), *The Letters of John Keats* (Oxford, Oxford University Press, 1952), 334–5.
7   John Hick, *Death and Eternal Life* (London, Macmillan, 1976), part V.
8   Keith Ward, *The Battle for the Soul* (London, Hodder, 1985), 149–50.
9   2 Samuel 14:14, Job 20:7, Genesis 2:7, Isaiah 14:11.
10 Job 42: 1–5.

11 Dan Cohn Sherbok, 'Death and immortality in the Jewish tradition', in P. and L. Badham, op. cit., 34.

12 Cohn Sherbok, op. cit., 26.

13 Sulayman Nyang, 'The teaching of the Qur'ān concerning life after death', in P. and L. Badham, op. cit., 72.

14 Qur'ān 21:16–17.

15 Salih Tug, 'Death and immortality in Islamic thought', in P. and L. Badham, op. cit., 87–8.

16 Edward Conze, *Buddhist Scriptures* (Harmondsworth, Penguin, 1959), 221.

17 Cited in W. Rahula, *What the Buddha Taught* (Bedford, Group Press, 1959), 59.

18 Derek Parfit, *Reasons and Persons* (Oxford, Oxford University Press, 1986).

19 John Hick, 'Response', in Stephen Davis, *Death and Afterlife* (London, Macmillan, 1989), 178.

20 Cited in F. Copleston, *History of Philosophy* (New York, Image Books, 1963), III, part 2, p.145.

12
Dying and living: some contemporary philosophical considerations

JOHN DANIEL

This chapter discusses two issues, or perhaps two sets of issues. The first concerns what I call our consciousness of death as such: is there such a phenomenon, and is there reason to fear death as such? The second concerns the contribution that a person's death, the way he or she dies, can make to our judgement on his or her life as a whole.

Death will be discussed throughout as *the coming to an end of a human life*. It is true that, as a consequence, attitudes towards death as a turning-point in life will be excluded. But attitudes towards death as an ending can overlap with attitudes towards it as a turning-point. For even if death is a turning-point, something comes to an end in it; and if it is a turning-point, it is one that can arouse emotions such as fear and apprehension even in believers.

1

Every one of us knows, in some sense, that he or she will die one day; and it is often claimed that one of the principal signs or effects of that knowledge is the fear of death. But this specification of the fear may conceal differences.

Sometimes an individual knows that he or she is going to die, in the sense of knowing that some process has begun that will cause death within a fairly definite period of time. This knowledge usually involves a belief about how he or she will die – that is, about what will cause this life to come to an end. On such occasions fear, and the effort to overcome fear, are familiar phenomena although it is worth bearing in mind that other emotions, such as anger and despair, are just as common. But there is a difference between such knowledge and my knowledge that I will die one day. This latter form of knowledge contains no reference to a specific causal process or to a fairly definite period of time. In the light of this distinction, many have claimed that the bare idea that I will die one day is capable of arousing in me emotions and attitudes such as fear, anger or despair. Accepting that such emotional phenomena do occur, I will say that their object is *death as such*. Writers about attitudes to death have always tended to concentrate on the response of fear, and I will do the same in what follows.

Freud noted phenomena that, in his opinion, reveal the fear of death as such (although he does not use that expression).[1] For example, even though we say that *everyone* dies, we behave as if it were not true. In a period of peace everybody is very reluctant to recognize explicitly and sincerely that he or she will die one day. Freud concluded that on the unconscious level we all believe ourselves immortal. And although we say that everybody *must* die, our conduct says otherwise. For we pay particular attention to any factor that can make a particular death appear to be accidental; and after someone's death we praise that individual as if dying as he or she did were a great achievement. Our general fear of death also comes out in our reluctance to take mortal risks, an attitude that limits the alternative courses of action that we are willing to consider seriously, and leads to unadventurous, superficial and boring lives. The value of these arguments varies. For example, holding that everyone must die (that is, some day, somehow), is perfectly consistent with holding that it was an accident that so-and-so died when he did, or that dying as he did (bravely, with dignity, and so on) was admirable.

Although it seems to be obvious that people do fear death as such, some philosophers have argued that such an emotion is, strictly speaking, impossible. For philosophical reasons, death cannot be the true object of the fear in those experiences that we misdescribe it as 'fearing death as such' – even though the true object is linked to death in a specific way. One philosopher who has argued thus is James Van Evra.[2]

The core of Van Evra's argument is his definition of death as *absence of experiences*. If death is the absence of experiences, it is not an object of consciousness, and consequently we cannot fear it. But this reasoning is already not probative. For it relies on the principle that nothing can be an object of consciousness unless it is a possible experience. This principle is contradicted by numerous counter-examples. If I see a table, the table is an object of consciousness for me even though being a table is not a possible experience for me. Perhaps the closest that I could get to this experience would be to experience being *used as* a table, as happened to servants formerly in the royal court of Thailand.

But this simple objection is also simplistic. After all, Van Evra is discussing the state described (loosely, in his view) as the individual's fear of his or her own death. And it is plausible enough to say that no one can fear some fate that cannot be imagined as befalling one. But in order for his overall conception of the way in which death enters consciousness to work, Van Evra needs a more restrictive claim: that no one can fear any fate such that he or she cannot imagine *from the inside* what it would be like to suffer it. If this claim is accepted, then of course the overall conception succeeds, since it would be self-contradictory to offer an insider's description, as it were, of a state defined as being without an inside. If there is an insider's description in this area, then, according to Van Evra, it is the description of the *process of dying*. When we speak of fearing death as such, what we are really speaking about is the fear of this process as such. The correct expression of this fear is not 'One day I will die,' but 'One day I will be dying'.

But if nobody can imagine his or her death in the sense that nobody can imagine, from the inside, himself or herself being dead, then what is the sense of the expression 'the process of dying' when we speak, as Van Evra does, of fearing the process of dying as such? For everyone who experiences that fear fears the process of his or her own dying. Van Evra deals with the problem by using Wittgenstein's remark, 'our life has no end in just the way in which our visual field has no limit'.[3] We cannot see the limit of our visual field, since seeing something implies locating it *within* the limits of our life. As Wittgenstein said in the same passage, 'Death is not an event in life: we do not live to experience death.'

Van Evra's point about the limit of our experiences may be put thus: the limit of our experiences is something other than the first state that we cannot experience after we have lived; rather, the limit is present, as it were, *in* some of our experiences. For example, as I read the letters on an optician's chart, beginning with the largest and moving towards the smallest, I come closer and closer to the limit of my ability to recognize the letters, and I know it. How do I know it? Not, absurdly, by comparing in my mind the size of the letters I recognize with the size of the first letter I cannot recognize. I know it by virtue of the increasing difficulty of recognizing the letters I do recognize. It is this progressive feature of each successive experience that produces the concept of a limit, of a letter that is too small for me to recognize, and not any impossible direct experience of such a letter. As the sick individual weakens, his or her experience is of coming closer and closer to the limit of all conscious powers. It is the experience of a comprehensive and progressive weakening that produces the concept of the limit of all experience. When we speak of fearing death as such, the true object of our fear is the process of dying as such – that is, a series of experiences that tends towards the cessation of all experience, as towards a limit.

According to Van Evra's argument, accordingly, we acquire the concept of death that enters into the experience we misdescribe as 'fearing death as such' by a process of extrapolation from a specific sort of series of experiences. Just as scientists construct the concept of zero force on the basis of the concept of diminishing force, so the ordinary individual can construct the concept of death, of maximum weakness, on the basis of increasing weakness. Our fear of death is to be totally reduced to our fear of the sorts of processes of which death is the limit.

Now any account of the fear of death must explain why we are so much more disturbed if we believe that we are dying than if we merely believe that our consciousness is getting feebler.[4] 'I am dying' is not equivalent to 'I am moving in the direction of death.' For the former, but not the latter, is contradicted by 'But I will recover.' And it will not help Van Evra to say that 'I am dying' is equivalent to 'I am moving in the direction of death and I will get there.' For his whole analysis of death as a limit was inspired by our inability to imagine, from inside, being dead; so that, from his standpoint, talk about arriving there ought to be equally unintelligible in this context.

In any case, it seems mistaken to link emotions in general with the power of imagining from inside what it would be like to do or to be done to thus and thus. The link will be most plausible if we take it that the thesis is that my experiencing fear, for example, necessarily involves my imagining, from inside, myself suffering some harm. But if brute animals can feel fear, does that state involve their imagining anything, whether from inside or outside? If, in order to minimize areas of conceptual disagreement, we stick to the case of human fear, then we ought to bear in mind that my fear can involve my thinking of something as dangerous to me, and that whereas such thinking may take an imaginative form, it does not have to. Neither is it plausible to argue that a fear, to count as an emotion, must be imaginative: in my terror, I may be far too preoccupied in avoiding the source of danger to have any capacity left for imagining what would happen to me if I failed.

I conclude that this attempt to show that there is not, strictly speaking, such a thing as fearing death as such is a failure. We are free to discuss some familiar facts without being made to doubt whether we are describing them correctly. For example, as was said above, our attitude towards a series of experiences changes radically if we believe that they will culminate in death. Thomas Nagel has said, ' . . . I should not really object to dying if it were not followed by death.'[5] Another phenomenon: occasionally the idea that he or she will die one day comes to a person's mind with shocking and frightening force. It cannot be held that this effect always derives from ideas present in the experience about when, or in what way, he or she will die. Some might object, holding that in such an experience thoughts about the proximity of death, or about the pain of a specific way of dying, affect us from an unconscious or subconscious level. But even so, Nagel's point would retain its force: would these subterranean thoughts be as powerful if they weren't thoughts involving *death*? They would not; and that is enough to show that thinking 'I will die' makes an essential contribution to the fear.

Let us accordingly accept that there are such phenomena as attitudes and emotions whose object is death as such. The one that has attracted most attention of the *fear* of death as such. But this fear can seem hard to understand: what is there to fear in death, if death is non-existence?

Centuries ago Epicurus argued that there was nothing to fear in death: 'Therefore . . . death is nothing to us, seeing that when we exist death is not present, and when death is present we do not exist.'[6] The argument is a dilemma: either we are dead or alive. If we are alive, death is not present (to us); and if we are dead, we are not there for anything to be present to us. But what worries people is not that death *is* not present, but that death *will* be present. The argument as a whole is ruined by Epicurus' failure to see that the non-being to come is present to people, in the sense that they suppose that, death being non-being, they have reason to fear it.

But although Epicurus' argument fails as a reasoned attempt to assuage the fear of death as such, his follower Lucretius made a point that enables more light to be thrown on the nature of this fear, as Nagel has pointed out.[7] Arguing that non-existence is nothing to fear, Lucretius claimed that, if the fear of death as such is the fear of non-existence, then we ought to find our ante-natal non-existence just as disturbing as our post-mortem non-existence. This is an important point; but the right conclusion to draw is that *ceasing to be* is what we fear in fearing death as such, not that the fear of death as such is irrational. If so, then understanding this fear depends on understanding what there is to fear in ceasing to be as such. I begin with some points made by Thomas Nagel.[8]

Nagel says that death is a misfortune to a man because it deprives him of his life, not because it is the beginning of a specific state of that man. For him, the essential misfortune is the loss, not what follows the loss. If we saw the state of being dead as a misfortune, we would have to say that Shakespeare is more unfortunate than Proust, since he has been dead for centuries rather than decades.

Explaining the misfortune of death in terms of the life of which the dead individual was deprived raises a problem, says Nagel, about the death of old people. Keats's death at twenty-five was more of a loss to Keats than Tolstoy's death at eighty-two was to Tolstoy, because the possibilities of continued life were so different in the two cases. If so, was dying such a loss to Tolstoy?

Nagel deals with the problem by a change of perspective. If we consider Tolstoy's death from outside, it seems that it was not much of a loss to him, because he would not have lived much longer anyway. But if we consider his death from his point of view, from inside, things look very different. Nagel says:

A man's sense of his own experience . . . does not embody this idea of a natural limit. His existence defines for him an essentially open-ended possible future, containing the same mixture of goods and evils he has found so tolerable in the past . . . he finds himself the subject of a *life*, with an indeterminate and not essentially limited future. Viewed in this way, death, no matter how inevitable, is an abrupt cancellation of indefinitely extensive possible goods.[9]

This account of how an individual conceives the misfortune of death relies on a notion of a possible future of which he or she will be deprived. The continuation of life is, in the individual's outlook, a possibility in the sense of being imaginable or conceivable without contradicting the descriptions under which he or she has always or mostly found her activities to be worthwhile in some sense or other. One might say that it is the sort of possibility that corresponds to 'I could go on doing this for ever', said as an expression of satisfaction. But all that needs to be said here is that an individual may think of his or her activities as worthwhile in ways that do not imply indefinite extensibility. For example, one might think of one's life in terms of a set of purposes such that, if they have been achieved, there is no longer any need to go on living. The *Nunc Dimittis*[10] is an expression of an attitude of this general type, which may also take non-religious forms: for example, people might feel that they had lived too long, in the sense that they no longer had a role in their community, whose life had by now passed them by, owing to the rise of younger generations. Such a sense of relegation would, in a certain way, not be a merely contingent matter, but something that could not be altered without very profound changes in the subjects' conception of a worthwhile life. It is true that such attitudes imply a more global view on life than the attitude that Nagel describes, and that they can coexist with positive evaluations of activities that are not at all tightly integrated into them. Nevertheless, given the global perspective, such activities would be part of life's small change, and to wish for a continuation of life for their sakes would be at the least to undermine the original perspective.

In his description of the attitude for which death is necessarily a misfortune, Nagel says that a human being 'finds himself the subject of a *life*, with an indeterminate and not essentially limited future'.[11] Bernard Williams has discussed the question whether living for ever as an earthly being could satisfy any human desire.[12] At first sight it looks as if the answer must be positive, and for a simple reason. If we set aside cases where death is better than life for somebody, we can say that death is always a misfortune, because it is always better to live than to die. But doesn't that lead immediately to the conclusion that it is better to live always than to die?

It does not. The premise 'At any time, it is better to live than to die' does not entail 'It is better to live at all times than to die.' We see this if we compare the statement 'At any time it is pleasant to taste ice-cream (i.e. at that time)' with 'It is pleasant to taste ice-cream at all times.' The former does not entail the latter because tasting icecream at a particular time is not the same activity as tasting ice-cream at all times, or all the time. In the same way, the living referred to in the state 'At any time it is better to live than to die' is not living at all times, or living for ever. In the spirit of Nagel's approach, the statement may be rephrased as 'At any time it is better to live to do that which I want at that time to do than to die before I can do it'. This rephrasing brings out the point that my reason for living, that I now want to do such-and-such, does not commend to me a future beyond the end of the period required to fulfil my desire; it definitely does not commend to me an endless future.

Williams argues that we could not have a reason for living a human life for ever. It follows that our human life is meaningless unless we see it as something that will come to an end. If we think about it, we shall see that an endless life could not satisfy any desire present in beings such as we are. But what reasons does Williams have for maintaining this?

His argument refers to a play by the author Karel Capek, in which is shown the predicament of Elina Makropulos, who is 342 years old – or who, if we count in another way, has been forty-two years old for three centuries. By now her life is nothing but 'boredom, indifference and coldness'. There is no joy in her, and no difference for her between song and silence. Williams argues that her condition is necessary, in the sense that it is not possible to describe a human being who would not be affected in the same way by living for ever.

Williams's argument contains two themes, one concerning

boredom and the other the concept of character. To take boredom first: people get bored with doing the same thing over and over; and after a long enough period is that not what life would be for us? But this is too simple an argument. The boredom of repeating the same action depends on such factors as the nature of the action and the agent's freedom to decide when exactly it is repeated. It may be that intellectuals tend to overlook this because they are especially prone to think that the persistence of our interest in something depends on our ability to discover some new aspect of it each time we return to it. But it is not true that our interest in a familiar action or object is directed on each occasion at some new aspect of it. For example, someone might choose repeatedly to listen to the same piece of music, because it satisfies some desire or emotion that arises repeatedly in him or her. It might be objected that such a way of listening to the music is too passive to be called taking an interest in it. Even if this is right, it is not so intolerable an activity that it could be called boring. It is true that there is interest motivated by curiosity, which only novelty can satisfy; but it is not true that the only alternative is boredom.

The second theme in Williams's argument is that of character. If Elina Makropulos were to look back at the first three centuries of her life, she might see that in her relations with others she had been doing the same things over and over again. Numerous repetitions of the same sort of relationship would gradually transform what had originally been a matter of acting into a matter of accepting, of putting up with the same relationship, with the same limitations.

Williams's argument is very condensed, but I believe that it can be understood as follows: as Elina Makropulos goes through the same sort of relationship time and time again, she comes to foresee with increasing clarity how it will develop. Knowing that about herself, she comes to see her actions in a new light, as the actions of one who has submitted to a familiar set of limitations. Before they became so repetitive they expressed a desire for a relationship of the sort in question; but after a sufficient number of repetitions they express the resignation of one who has settled for an unimaginative routine.

But what, asks Williams, if she has never repeated the same relationship? Then it must be said that she has no settled character, and that no experience is very close to her heart; there is a distance between her and her actions.

So we see that Williams's question is this: for what sort of character could everlasting life be a worthwhile aim? If someone has a settled character, then continuing *for ever* to act in accordance with that character will bring a new and unfavourable self-assessment; and if he or she has no settled character, and consequently no comparatively specific set of values, to what part of him or her could living for ever appeal?

The first horn of this dilemma presupposes an individual who assesses his or her own character, as that is revealed by his or her actions. Not everybody is as self-conscious as this. It is true that Williams's question is, 'In the name of what could living for ever appear attractive to someone?', and that one *prima facie* possible answer could be 'In the name of the agent's self-image, of his or her conception of his or her character'. Williams argues against this reply, on the ground that endless repetition must change the self-image for the worse. But is that necessary? An agent who, on reflection, discovers that he or she is repeatedly doing the same sort of thing might think with some satisfaction that he or she has settled desires and reliable ways of implementing them. Williams would describe this as becoming resigned to one's limitations. It is true that the thought 'It will be different this time' will become increasingly difficult to take seriously. But why must 'It will be rather like last time?' *necessarily* be a lowering thought? It seems that it would be necessarily so only for one who values novelty as such. But such a relativized necessity is much weaker than the position Williams originally defended.

I conclude from this discussion that Nagel has not shown that the ways in which we conceive of our life and activities are necessarily such that, if our life is not intolerable, death will appear as a deprivation of the greatest good then available to us; and that Williams has not shown that there is no reflective attitude within which everlasting life could be desired by its human subject.

2

In our culture much attention is paid to the way a person dies – not to the sorts of facts that are recorded on a death certificate, but to the moral character of the death. We often ask whether somebody died honourably or shamefully, defiantly or submissively, in agony of mind or peacefully, and so on. We think that the answers to these questions are important, and it is natural to suppose that the reason for this is the contribution they make to our view of the life and character of the person in question. Until we get answers we feel incapable of saying what kind of life that person had led, or what kind of person he or she was. But the question that now arises is *how* those terminal events contribute to our understanding of the entire life and character.

Let us note first a possibility illustrated by Tolstoy's well-known story 'The death of Ivan Illich'. The story shows how Ivan Illich comes to terms with the fact that he will very shortly die. Tolstoy describes the turning-point in Ivan Illich's attitude to his death as follows: '. . . It was revealed to him that even though his life had not been what it should have been it was still possible to rectify it.' I begin with the assumption that the possibility revealed to Ivan Illich was the possibility of rectifying his entire life, including his past. Taking the assumption to be true, the problem would be to understand the sense of 'rectify' in this context. Was Tolstoy suggesting that if Ivan Illich had not experienced his conversion, his life up to the time at which, as it happened, his conversion occurred would have been morally defective, but that since he actually did experience a conversion his previous life was not defective in that way? It is important to avoid two misunderstandings here. It is not being suggested that Ivan Illich's conversion retrospectively caused a real change in his earlier life. On the other hand, it is not enough to say that it is our judgement on the earlier life that is rectified, by virtue of the fact that the conversion draws our attention to something that was there already but unnoticed by us. The expression 'rectifying his life' suggests that after the conversion something was true of the earlier life that would not otherwise have been so. But whatever this new truth may be, if it does not imply that the earlier life was morally defective, then the conversion cannot be described in terms of rectifying a life that had not been what it should have been.

Could it be said that the rectification in question is a matter of *compensating for* the selfishness of the earlier life? The suggestion would be that Ivan Illich's acceptance of his death outweighs all his previous faults, so that the overall value of his life is positive.

We would have to take into account some incommensurable items in trying to strike this balance. But even if that were possible in this case at least, to talk of compensation would be unconvincing. We would be talking of balancing a lifetime of selfishness against a few minutes of acceptance, an acceptance that no one else knows about and which cannot lead to any external manifestation. How would that acceptance be enough to rectify the earlier life in the sense now in question?

The importance of the way in which death is faced might be approached in terms of a specific ideal. For example, the *Iliad* and the early Welsh *Gododdin* describe societies that set a very high value on courage. Courage is the virtue displayed in facing danger, and it follows that the way in which death is faced in battle will be among the most important criteria of a man's courage and worth. It is entirely understandable why Homer, and to a lesser extent the poet of the *Gododdin*, both give detailed accounts of the ways in which men fight, kill and are killed. These actions are the severest tests of their value.

Could a similar approach be taken in the case of Ivan Illich? Could we say that the way in which he died was a test of his character, in the same way as a soldier's death in battle? The difficulty here is that there is no virtue or social role to link Ivan Illich's death in the appropriate way with his earlier life. He was a civil servant. It may be that a civil servant's duties would oblige him or her, in extreme circumstances, to suffer death. But being ready to face death is not a central feature of being a good civil servant as it is of being a good soldier. And in the particular case of Ivan Illich, no one could think that, by dying as he did, he was performing to the end his duty as a civil servant.

But although readiness to face death is not a typical feature of every virtue, is it not true that death is the severest test of any virtue, and not merely of soldierly virtue? Tolstoy's story suggests that the approach of death makes everybody introverted and self-centred. Consequently, to be able to give priority, as death approaches, to the needs and rights of others, as Ivan Illich did, is highly virtuous. Dying well in this sense is a moral triumph, and dying badly a moral failure. Such ideas create the possibility of giving a new sense to talk of rectifying a life. If Ivan Illich's earlier life has led to his conversion and unselfish death, may it not be said that his life is thereby changed? Without the conversion, his earlier life would have been an uninspiring series of selfish acts; but given the conversion we might describe it as perhaps an apprenticeship. Similarly, on the basis of later developments, Giotto is called the precursor of the humanist art of the Renaissance. Without those developments the description would be false.

Even if all this is admitted, it still does not generate an appropriate sense of 'rectify'. If Giotto was a precursor, it is partly by virtue of an appropriate relation between him and later artists. But there is nothing to link Ivan Illich's conversion with his earlier life, except his bare human identity. He had not striven to live in accordance with virtues that are specially linked with facing death. Indeed, strictly speaking, he had no virtues at all. He was a selfish man who was less repellent than many of his kind because of his reluctance to quarrel. Even though accepting his death was the best thing he had ever done, doing so was not the climax of his earlier life, so that he did not thereby rectify his life in the relevant sense. There is no suitable relation between his conversion and the moral history that preceded it.

In the light of all this, it cannot be said that the rectification mentioned by Tolstoy refers to Ivan Illich's entire life. We ought rather to say that Ivan Illich intends to rectify what remains of his life. He remains a person who lived the greater part by far of his life in selfishness and who experienced a deathbed conversion. I do not want to suggest that the event was unimportant. It is rather that its importance is neither retrospective nor prospective but lies rather in the inherent value of an unselfish view and in the special obstacles that the consciousness of imminent death creates for the achievement of such a view.

Notes

An earlier version of this paper was published (in Welsh) in *Efrydiau Athronyddol*, LIII (1990).

1   In his essay 'Thoughts for the times on war and death' (1915), in his *Collected Papers* (London, Hogarth Press, 1950), IV, 287–317.

2   In his article 'On death as a limit', in J. Donnelly (ed.), *Language, Metaphysics and Death* (New York, Fordham University Press, 1978), 25–31.

3   L. Wittgenstein, *Tractatus Logico-Philosophicus*, tr. D. F. Pears and B.
    F. McGuiness (London, Routledge and Kegan Paul, 1963), 6.4311.
4   For the source of this thought, see n.5 below.
5   In his article 'Death', in his *Mortal Questions* (Cambridge, CUP,
    1979), 3n.
6   From his 'Letter to Menoeceus': Diogenes Laertius, *Lives of the
    Eminent Philosophers*, X.125; transl. A. A. Long and D. Sedley, *The
    Hellenistic Philosophers* (Cambridge, CUP, 1987), I, 150.
7   Nagel, 'Death', 7–8; for Lucretius' point, see his *Nature of the
    Universe* (Harmondsworth, Penguin, 1951), 125.
8   Nagel, op. cit., 9.
9   Nagel, op. cit., 9–10.
10 Luke, 2:29–32.
11 Nagel, op. cit., 10.
12 'The Makropulos Case', in B. Williams, *Problems of the Self*
    (Cambridge, CUP, 1973), 82–100.

Index